Helping Children Know God

Compiled & Edited by
Christine Yount

Group®
Loveland, Colorado

Helping Children Know God

Credits
Contributing Authors: Katrina Arbuckle, Susan Grover, Sheila Halasz, Robyn Kundert, Ellen Larson, Pamela Montgomery, Cynthia Nelson, Walter Norvell, Linda Shepherd, Esther Stockwell, Heather Ward, and Michael Warden
Book Acquisitions Editor: Mike Nappa
Editors: Christine Yount and Candace McMahan
Senior Editor: Lois Keffer
Creative Products Director: Joani Schultz
Copy Editor: Bob Buller
Art Director: Helen H. Lannis
Cover Art Director: Liz Howe
Designer: Kathleen Kinkoff
Computer Graphic Artist: Bill Fisher
Cover Illustrator: Kathleen Kinkoff
Illustrator: Donna Nelson and Jim Connolly
Production Manager: Gingar Kunkel

Library of Congress Cataloging-in-Publication Data
Helping children know God / [contributing authors, Susan Grover...et al.].
     p. cm.
   Includes index.
   ISBN 1-55945-605-1
   1. Christian education of children.   2. God—Study and teaching.   I. Grover, Susan.
II. Group Publishing.

10 9 8 7 6 5 4 3   04 03 02 01 00 99 98 97
Printed in the United States of America.

Contents

Introduction

If you were to ask me or any other children's worker why we are involved in children's ministry, most of us would probably reply, "to help children know, love, and follow God." Yet in the midst of planning programming, preparing curriculum, and managing the classroom, that goal often gets pushed aside.

It happened in my Sunday school class recently. I had been teaching the children about the Ten Commandments—the "Thou shalts" and "Thou shalt nots." Finally, after teaching the fifth commandment and trying to review the four before it, I began to wonder: "What is really getting through to these children?" If my class were the only exposure they'd ever have to God's Word, would they learn—like many people today—that God is a God of rules who cares more about what they do than who they are? Or would they learn that God is a loving God who wants to enter into relationship with them so they can know him?

I feared they were learning the first lesson . . . and it troubled me.

Hence the need for this book, *Helping Children Know God*. I've longed to finish editing it—primarily because I can't wait to use the activities to help the kids in my class learn about this awesome God we serve. (How nice it would have been to use an activity on God's goodness to help them understand why he lovingly made the Ten Commandments to protect us!) And I've also looked forward to sharing this book with all of you who have likewise struggled to find creative and effective ways to teach children about God.

In this book you'll find a collection of activities, games, crafts, field trips, service projects, and more that'll help you clearly teach about 11 attributes of God. You can use these pick-and-choose ideas to build a meeting around one character trait of God, or you can use the ideas to supplement the curriculum you're already using. Use the Scripture Index (pp. 110-111) to identify activities that teach your Bible verse(s).

I know you want children to know God and enter into a deeper relationship with him. If you didn't, you wouldn't be reading this. So however you choose to use this book, my prayer is that you'll find it to be a valuable tool to help children begin a lifelong search to know God.

"So let us know, let us press on to know the Lord. His going forth is as certain as the dawn; and he will come to us like the rain, like the spring rain watering the earth" (Hosea 6:3, NASB).

Press on!

Christine Yount, Editor

Chapter One

Who Is God?

How do you act when you meet someone for the first time? Are you a little nervous? What do you say? What questions do you ask? How do you form first impressions?

A primary goal of children's ministry is to introduce children to God. God is a personal being whom they can know. However, before we focus on specific attributes of God, it's important to help children understand the different ways they can get to know God.

Kids may be a little nervous about studying who God is. They're not sure what questions to ask. In addition, they may have already formed false impressions about God that you'll need to explore and correct. Use this chapter to introduce children to God and help them be comfortable with learning more about God.

● ● ●

By What Name?

Have children sit in a circle. Introduce yourself to the group by telling your full name and a nickname that you like.

Form trios. Have kids tell each other their names and nicknames. Then have trios work together to think of different names we call God, such as Father, Creator, Lord, Holy One, Almighty, or Yahweh. After one minute, have kids call out the names they thought of for God. After children respond, read aloud Exodus 3:11-15. Then ask:

● **If you were to choose a name for yourself, what would you choose? Why?**

● **How do the names for God that you thought of describe who God is?**

● When you talk to God, what name do you use most frequently? Why?

Say: **Every person has a name. Often the first thing we need to learn about a person is his or her name. In the same way, God is a person, and he wants us to begin to know him by learning his names.**

Freedom Fighter

Play this game outdoors after dark or in a darkened room. Choose two or three players to be the "enemy" and one player to be the "freedom fighter." When an enemy tags one of the other players, that player must stand motionless until the freedom fighter shines a flashlight beam on him or her. The light frees the player to continue the game.

After 10 minutes or when children tire of this game, have children sit in a circle.

Read aloud Psalm 27:1-3. Ask:

● **Who are our enemies?**

● **Should we be afraid of any enemy? Why or why not?**

● **How was this game like real life? How was it different?**

Read aloud John 1:1-5. Ask:

● **How is Jesus like a light in the darkness?**

● **How can Jesus' light help us?**

Say: **God provides his light through Jesus when we're afraid of our enemies. God protects us and takes care of us. God is a light in the darkness.**

Getting to Know You

Cut 3×5 cards in half. Write the names of Bible characters on separate cards. Tape a card to each child's forehead, but don't let children see the names written on their cards. Tell children to ask each other yes and no questions to discover the names on their foreheads. If someone cannot guess the name within five minutes, allow him or her to look in a mirror to figure out the name.

After children have discovered their names, ask:

● **What questions did you ask to discover your name?**

● **If you wanted to get to know someone, what questions would you ask that person?**

Form trios. Have kids discuss this question in their trios:

● What questions would you ask to learn who God is?

Say: **Even Jesus' disciples wanted to know more about God. Listen to this conversation between Jesus and a disciple named Philip.**

Read aloud John 14:9-11.

Say: **Just as we have to ask questions to get to know a new friend, we can ask questions to get to know God. And just as we see our names reflected when we look in the mirror, we see God's reflection when we look at Jesus. Jesus mirrors who God is. As we ask more questions about Jesus, we'll learn more about God because we see God when we look at Jesus.**

✗ I Am Adopted

Form pairs. Give each pair a bag of rice and set out glue, markers, yarn, and buttons. Have each pair create a "baby" out of the supplies and the bag of rice. Tell pairs to name and adopt their children. Have kids sit in a circle and tell the names of their babies.

Say: **Describe what you'll have to do to care for your adopted baby.**

After children respond, read aloud John 1:12-13. Then ask:

● **How does it make you feel to know that God has adopted you?**

● **What do you think it means for God to be our Father?**

Say: **In the same way that you created and adopted a child, God has created you and wants to adopt you as his child. If we believe in Jesus, God becomes our Father. He adopts us as his very own children.**

✗ I Want to Know You

Form groups of four. Have each group find a place quiet enough to work but close enough to the other groups to carry on a class discussion.

Say: **Let's take a moment to discover what we know about God. I'm going to start a sentence, then I'd like your foursome to work as a team to complete the sentence.**

Read aloud the following statements and give foursomes up to one minute to complete each statement. Have children call out their answers after time is up.

● **Some things that God does for us are…** Kids may say things such as "gives us rain" or "answers our prayers."

● **Some words that describe God are…** Kids may say things such as "loving," "kind," "wise," "gracious," "powerful," "forgiving," or "faithful."

● **God spends his time**... Kids may say "making things," "listening to our prayers," or "watching over us."

● **What God loves most is**... Kids may say "children," "the world," or "all people."

Say: **We can learn some things about God from each other, but reading the Bible is the best way to get to know God. Listen to what the Bible says about God.**

Read aloud Psalms 23:1-4; 66:3-4; and 86:6-10.

Say: **God is a loving God who is active in our lives. God loves us very much and wants us to know him. So God gave us the Bible to help us learn more about him.**

End the activity by encouraging children to read their Bibles during the upcoming week to discover one new thing about God. Ask kids to report their discoveries the next time you meet together.

✓ If I Were God

Form groups of four. Instruct each group to make at least five new, unheard-of, make-believe creatures out of modeling dough or clay. Have groups name their own creatures. After 15 minutes, have groups explain their creations to the rest of the class. Afterward, ask:

● **How did you like being the one who could create anything you wanted?**

● **In what ways are your creations like you? How are they different from you?**

● **How was this process similar to the way God created the world? How was it different?**

Say: **Listen to what Acts 17:24-28 says about how and why God created the world.** Read the verses, then ask:

● **Why did God create the things he did?**
● **How did God make us to be like him?**
● **How are we different from God?**
● **Why do you think God wants to be part of our lives?**
● **How can you let God be part of your life?**

Say: **God lovingly created everything. He cares about you and me and wants to be part of our lives. It's incredible that the Creator of the universe wants to be our friend.**

Meet My Friend

Ask:

● **When you make a new friend, what do you like to find out about that person right away?**

List kids' responses on a chalkboard or newsprint. Then have kids choose three items from the list that they'd like to have each person tell today.

Say: **Listen to what the Bible says about God.** Read aloud 2 Kings 19:14-16a.

Form trios. Have kids introduce themselves in their trios by saying: "The Lord is my God and I am (name), child of (parents' names)." Instruct them also to share the three pieces of information that the class chose from the list. After the trios finish their introductions, bring everyone together. Have each person introduce another trio member to the entire class, giving the same information. For example, someone might say, "This is Kelly. She is in the fifth grade, she likes to skate, and her favorite animal is a dog."

After everyone has been introduced, have kids return to their trios to develop a similar introduction for God. Say: **As you plan your introduction, think about questions such as**

● **Where does God live?**

● **What does God do in your life?**

● **What does God like to do?**

Say: **For example, you might say, "God lives in heaven, he provides a place for us to live, and he likes to listen to prayers."**

After kids are prepared, have each trio introduce God to the large group. After the introductions, ask:

● **What did you feel was the most important thing to share about God in your introduction?**

● **How can we learn more about who God is?**

Say: **There is so much to learn about God. We already know some things, but God wants us to learn even more.**

Mysterious Leader

Have kids sit on the floor in a circle with their legs crossed. Choose one volunteer to leave the room for two minutes. Select a "mysterious leader" from the group. Instruct children to imitate whatever the leader does, whether it be winking, scratching their heads, or something else. Every 30 seconds, the mysterious leader should change his or her movements without the volunteer noticing.

Have the volunteer come in, sit in the circle, and guess who the mysterious leader is. After the mysterious leader has been identified, repeat the game so other children may have the chance to be the volunteer or the mysterious leader.

Say: **Listen to how Jesus became a mysterious leader among us.** Read aloud John 1:14.

Say: **In this game, some of you didn't know who the mysterious leader was, but he or she was among you.** Ask:

● **How is God in our group at all times?**

● **Is it easy or difficult to know that God is present? Explain.**

● **How did you eventually find out who the mysterious leader was?**

● **Will the same method help you discover God among us? Why or why not?**

Say: **As we look for God's presence among us, we will find things all around us that point to him.**

Shout for the Lord

Have kids sit on the floor in a circle. Then blindfold each child.

Say: **We're going to shout with joy to God. You'll say "Praise the Lord" into this tape recorder. But first, please be silent for a while as I rearrange you.**

Rearrange children so they don't know who's sitting beside them. Then approach each child and have him or her "praise the Lord" into the tape recorder. Write children's names in the order they record. Continue until all the children have recorded their voices.

Rearrange the children again, then have them remove their blindfolds. Rewind and play the tape. Have children guess whose voice is whose.

Say: **Listen to what the Bible says about how we can tell if we're God's sheep.**

Then read aloud John 10:14-16. Ask:

● **Was it easy or difficult to identify other people's voices? Explain.**

● **Is it easy or difficult to identify God's voice? Explain.**

● **How can you be sure you hear God's voice?**

Say: **As we get to know God better through his Word, we'll be better able to identify his voice. And when we know his voice, we'll follow him more closely.**

A Strong Tower

Say: **In Bible times, people built strong walls to protect themselves. They also built high towers inside of the walls so that even if the walls were broken the people in the towers would always be safe. Let's play a game to see what it would've been like to live in a city with a strong tower.**

Have children form a circle, link arms, and face outward. Put a block tower in the middle of the circle to represent a strong tower for the people living in the city. Try to roll a beach ball or kickball through the children's legs to knock down the tower. The children can gently kick the ball away if it comes near them.

After everyone has had at least one turn kicking the ball away, read aloud Psalm 61:1-3. Ask:

● **How did you feel when the ball went through your legs? when you stopped the ball?**

● **How well did our tower stand against the attacks from the ball?**

● **Why does the Bible say God is like a strong tower?**

● **How does God act like a strong tower in our lives?**

Have each child build a tower out of sugar cubes and glue. Children can also make fences with glued-together craft sticks or toothpicks stuck together with small marshmallows. Glue the towers and fences to cardboard for stability. Have children take their projects home to remind them that God is their strong tower who will always protect them. (Note: If you use nonedible materials such as glue in the fences, remind children not to eat their creations.)

Take Your Shoes Off

Tape four pieces of newsprint to the floor to form a square. Place a large plant in the middle of the square to represent the burning bush. Have children sit along the edges of the square.

Say: **Let's learn about how God spoke to Moses in a special way.** Read aloud Exodus 3:1-6. Ask:

● **Why did Moses have to remove his shoes?**

Encourage each child to share a word that describes God. After everyone has shared, have children record their responses on the newsprint in front of them (help younger children write). Pour red, yellow, and orange tempera paint into separate pie pans. Have each child use a paintbrush to completely cover the bottom of one foot with paint. Then have each child make a footprint beside his or her written characteristic of God. Ask:

● **Which of these words describing God makes you feel safe?**

● **Which words don't you understand?**

● **Which words about God are the most important to you right now? Explain.**

Say: **Even though we may not understand everything about God, we can know for sure that he loves us!**

EXTRA MILE IDEA

Perfect Agreement ✓

Establish an obstacle course in a nearby park. For example, have kids go around a tree, under a swing, over a merry-go-round twice, and so on to return to the starting place. Be sure to choose safe and easy obstacles.

Form trios. Have kids in each trio link arms to form a small circle, facing outward. Have trios move through the obstacle course with their arms linked. Trios must begin again if their arms become unlinked. Afterward, ask:

● **What was it like moving through the obstacle course with your partners?**

● **How did your partners help you get back to the starting point?**

Say: **Just as there were three of you teamed up in this game, there are three persons in God—God the Father, God the Son, and God the Holy Spirit.**

Read aloud 2 Corinthians 13:14. Say: **God the Father, God the Son, and God the Holy Spirit work together.** Ask:

● **How is this like how your trio worked together during the game?**

● **How is this different from how your trio worked together?**

Say: **It's hard to understand how God can be three persons and still be one God. But that's what the Bible tells us about God. As you grow as a Christian, God can help you understand more about how he can be the Father, Son, and Holy Spirit all at once.**

Chapter Two

Our All-Powerful God

Children today are surrounded by images of power. They've seen the results of powerful bombs. They experience the terrifying power of storms, floods, and fires. And they usually have a favorite powerful hero, whether real or imagined. Children need to understand that God's power is much greater than any power they've ever experienced or even thought about.

Kids' fears are just as real and terrifying to them as fears of losing a job or a loved one are to adults. When they're afraid to walk to school past bullies...when it's dark outside and lonely inside...when the world seems out of control...children need to know that our omnipotent, living God has the same  power today that he had to create the world, part the Red Sea, and heal the blind man sitting by the pool of Bethzatha. Use this chapter to introduce children to their powerful God.

● ● ●

I Am Made Strong

Form pairs. Have partners tell each other one way they've seen people demonstrate power. Responses may range from picking up something heavy to being the leader. Ask:
- Do you think you're powerful? Why or why not?
- How do people become powerful?

Say: **Many people use money or different kinds of exercise to become strong and powerful, but I'm going to show you a way to become powerful with no money and without exercising.** Ask:
- If your partner put a finger on his or her head, do you think

you would have enough power to pull the finger away? That seems like it would be very easy.

In the pairs, have one child put an index finger on top of his or her head and hold it there tightly. Then have that child's partner try to pull it away with a steady pull—no jerking or pushing. (Children will find that it's not as easy as they think to pull one small finger.) Have children switch places so everyone gets a chance to pull. Show that even an adult like you has difficulty pulling away someone else's finger. Ask:

● **Did you think your one small finger could be so strong? Why or why not?**

Say: **Listen to what the Bible says about people who are strong.** Read aloud Psalm 1:1-3.

Say: **The Bible says that when you live a life that honors and pleases God, God strengthens you with his great power. God puts strength not only in your finger but also in your whole body every day. God can produce all kinds of miracles, but one of the most powerful things God does is give you power to live a good life.**

Let's pray: Dear God, thank you for all the powerful things you've done in the world. (Mention positive things children mentioned at the beginning.) **Thank you also for the power you give us each day to do the things that are right. This week, each one of us is going to do something nice for someone else. I'm going to be friendly to someone I don't know.** (Go around the room and let everyone add something.) **We know you'll always strengthen us with power when we need it most. In Jesus' name, amen.**

Say: **Show your "strong finger" to your parents or a friend. And remember, we have power because we have a big and powerful God.**

Masters and Slaves

Form pairs and have partners face each other. Say: **We're going to play Masters and Slaves. A master has the power to ask a slave to do almost anything, to jump up and down or tie the master's shoelaces, for example. The slave has to obey the order immediately.**

Have partners choose who'll be the master first. Tell children not to command each other to do anything embarrassing or dangerous. Have the master order the slave to do things for two minutes. Then direct kids to exchange roles for two more minutes. Gather kids together and ask:

● **As a master, did you feel powerful? Explain.**
● **As a slave, did you feel powerless? Explain.**

Say: **Let's see what the Bible says about God's power.** Then read aloud Isaiah 40:10-11. Ask:

● Is God like the masters in this game? Why or why not?

● What are the differences between God's power and human power?

● How well did the slaves obey the masters in this game?

● How should we obey our all-powerful God?

Have kids rejoin their partners. Encourage them to pray and ask God for power in an area in which they feel weak.

After kids finish praying, read aloud Philippians 4:13. Say: **God is powerful. God will give you his power when you feel weak.**

Mirror, Mirror

Form pairs. Have partners do the Mirror Mime. Have each pair choose a leader and a follower. Explain that the leaders are to mime actions and the followers are to copy those actions exactly as if they were images in a mirror. After two minutes, have the leaders and followers change roles. Continue for another two minutes. Then ask:

● How did you like being the leader? the follower?

● What kind of power did the leader have?

● What might've happened if you hadn't followed your leader's movements?

Say: **The Bible is full of stories that show Jesus' power. Listen to this story.**

Read aloud Mark 4:35-41. Ask:

● What happened in this story to show that Jesus, as God's Son, had unusual power?

● Do you know anyone else who's powerful enough to do this?

● Can God use his power to change people, or do we only see God's power in things such as storms?

● If God can make anyone and everything do exactly as he likes, why doesn't he make us do all the things we should?

● Since we know that God doesn't make us into robots, what does that tell us about what God is like?

Say: **God has the power to do anything he wants, but God doesn't make us follow him, because he wants us to follow him out of love.**

Power Plant

Have kids each turn to a person close to them and answer these questions:

- Who is the most powerful person in the world?
- What's the most powerful force in the world?

Say: **Now tell your partner why you think the powerful person and force are powerful.**

After kids have had time to answer, say: **Listen to what the Bible says about God's power.**

Read aloud 1 Chronicles 29:11-12. Say: **These verses say that God can do all these things because of his power. They also teach that God is all-powerful. We could say that God is the power plant. Can someone tell me what a power plant is?**

Say: **Let's pretend this yarn is a wire from the power plant to us.**

Form a half-circle. Give each child an arm's length piece of yarn. As children hold one end of their yarn pieces, stand in the opening of the half-circle and hold the other ends of the yarn pieces. Say: **Name something that needs power to work.**

As each person responds with an idea, ask him or her what the source of that power is. Then ask what the source of that power is. Continue until you trace every powerful thing back to the ultimate source of power—God. For example, if someone names a television, trace it back to electricity, which is often generated by either wind or water, both of which God made.

After everyone has had a chance to name something, have children continue to hold on to their ends of the yarn while you hold on to the other ends. Have kids walk clockwise, raising and lowering their yarn pieces and saying, "Power, power, God is all power. Yea, God!"

Say: **All power comes from God. Just as our yarn connected you to me, we need to stay connected to God through our faith in him.**

Power Tag

Play this game outside or in a large open space. Choose one or two children to be chasers who pursue the rest of the class. In order to be "safe," kids must freeze and call out the name of a powerful machine. After five seconds, they must move again. If kids can't think of a powerful machine in time, they're tagged and must then take the place of the chasers.

Give kids time to think of machines before the game begins. After five minutes, change the rules. This time kids must call out something powerful that God has created in nature. For example, kids might name earthquakes, tornadoes, rivers, or tigers.

After five minutes, ask:

● **How many things does God give power to?**

Read aloud Matthew 28:18-20. Remind kids that God gives Christians the power of the Holy Spirit so they can become part of God's power team.

Pushover

Form pairs. Have partners stand, face each other, and place the palms of their hands together. Tell children they must try to push the other person off balance without moving their feet. Whoever moves a foot is out and must sit down and watch. Demonstrate how partners can try to push each other off balance and consider grouping children by grades or sizes to keep a small child from being overwhelmed. Repeat this process by having the winning children find partners and play again.

After this game, ask:

● **Who is the strongest person in our group?**

● **How does our strength and power compare to God's strength and power?**

● **Does our powerful God try to push us around? Explain.**

● **How does God use his power?**

Say: **Let's read about how God uses his power.**

Read aloud Psalm 147:1-5. Ask:

● **What do these verses say that God uses his power for?**

● **What is one way you'd like God to use his power to help you?**

After children answer, lead them in prayer, using their ideas as prayer requests.

Rain Band

Create instruments for a musical thunderstorm. You'll need flashlights for bursts of lightning, two boards to slap together to make the crack of lightning, and pie tins to tap fingers on to make the sound of rain. Make thunder by shaking a large piece of bendable metal, pounding on a large cardboard box, or stamping feet on the floor. Make wind sounds by having children whistle or blow across the top of empty bottles, beginning with bottles with lower pitches and proceeding to bottles with higher pitches. Assign children to play different instruments. Have kids sit with others playing the same instruments.

Say: **Now it's time for the storm to begin. Let's have the rain begin quietly.** (Have children drum their fingers on pie tins.) **Now the rain is getting louder. Let the lightning crack.** (Have children with the boards slap them together.) **And now let the thunder roll!** (Have kids make thunder sounds.)

Continue calling out the sounds of the storm in different patterns. Go from loud crashes and lots of rain down to the gentle splish splash of a morning rain. Have a tree get hit by lightning, making the sounds of the crack of the wood and the crash as the tree hits the ground. Have everyone "whisper" the sound of the leaves as they settle when the wind dies down.

Let children take turns conducting the "rain band." When everyone who would like to conduct has had a chance, form groups of four.

Say: **In your group, talk about the worst storm you can remember. Be sure to tell why it was the worst for you, then describe the power of God you felt in that storm.**

After five minutes, bring everyone together. Say: **The Bible tells us about several great storms, but today I'll be reading about the great storm and flood that God told Noah and his family to prepare for.**

Read aloud Genesis 7:11-24. Ask:
- **What do you think that rainstorm was like?**
- **How do you think Noah and his family felt?**
- **How would you feel if it were to rain for a long, long time?**
- **When Noah looked out on all that water, even after the storm had ended, what do you think he thought about God's power?**
- **Storms can be destructive. The one that caused Noah's flood certainly was! Where can we see God's power in a positive way?**

Say: **Storms are powerful, but God is even more powerful. And God wants to use his power to help us.**

Real Power

Form two teams. Have each team line up from one end of the room to the other. At the end of one line, place an adult with a manual can opener; at the same end of the other line, an adult with an electric can opener. Give the person at the other end of each line an unopened can of peaches. On "go," have kids pass the cans down the lines, get them opened by the adults, and pass them back to the beginning.

After this game, have the children sit down. Pour the peaches into small bowls, hand out spoons, and let children enjoy the peaches. Ask:

● **What was the biggest difference between each team's performance?**

● **If you were on the team with the manual can opener, what did you think as your can was being opened?**

● **If your team had the electric can opener, what did you think?**

● **Is God's power more like the manual can opener or the electric one? Explain.**

● **How is God's power different from ours?**

Read Colossians 1:16-17. Ask:

● **According to these verses, how far does God's power reach?**

● **What is one example of God's power?**

Say: **There are no limits to God's power. He can do anything he chooses to do.**

Shake, Rattle, and Roll

Form a large circle. Have kids think of powerful natural phenomena such as wind, rain, hail, earthquakes, lightning and thunder, tornadoes, and snowstorms. Go around the circle one at a time, having kids call out ways we see God's power in nature. Have everyone dramatize each natural force as it's named. For example, kids could shake for earthquakes, shiver for snow, twirl around for a tornado, slap their legs to make rain and hail sounds, stomp their feet for thunder, and whistle and whirl for the wind. It's OK if kids call out something already named.

Explain that when you shout, "Shake, rattle, and roll!" kids must do all the previous actions at once!

Once everyone has called out something and you've made the place shake, rattle, and roll two or three times, have kids sit on the floor.

Say: **Listen to how God can make the entire world shake, rattle, and roll.**

Read aloud Jeremiah 51:15-16. Then ask:

● **What does God have power over?**

● How do you feel about the way God uses his power?

Say: **God has power over everything. Sometimes we don't under-stand why God let's some things happen, but we can trust God because he loves us.**

Volcano Power

You'll need the following supplies for each trio of children: ½ cup vinegar, ¼ cup water, 3 tablespoons baking soda, a tall glass, a long-handled spoon, aluminum foil, 5 drops of liquid dish detergent, a large baking pan, and 3 drops of food coloring.

Form trios. Have each trio create a volcano by following these direc-tions: Set the glass right side up in the middle of the pan. Mold the foil around the glass to form the cone shape of a volcano. Put baking soda in the glass, then add dish detergent and food coloring. Gently pour in water, then stir lightly. Slowly pour vinegar into the volcano. Wait and watch what happens.

Say: **Listen to this verse to see if you can identify something that's too difficult for God to do.**

Have a volunteer read aloud Jeremiah 32:17. Ask:

● **Is God more powerful than an explosive volcano? Why or why not?**

● **How would you describe God's power?**

● **What kinds of things can God do because he's all-powerful?**

Say: **God can do anything, so we can trust God to help us when we need his power.**

Wacky Wrestling Game

Form pairs. Have partners face each other across a table. Say: **We're going to try an elbow wrestling contest. Place your right elbows on the table. On the count of three, press your elbow against your partner's and try to push your partner's elbow off the table top.**

Afterward, say: **Listen to what God's Word says about God's strength.**

Read aloud Isaiah 50:2. Ask:

● **How does it feel to be strong?**

● **Do you think God has to wrestle to prove that he is the strongest? Why or why not?**

● **Is there anyone who's stronger than God? Explain.**

Say: **Most of us have found that no matter how strong we are, someone else always seems to be stronger. In the same way that we sometimes have to prove to others that we're strong, God sometimes shows us that he's strong so we'll believe in him. If you doubt that God is strong, remember some of the powerful miracles he has done in the past.**

Invite kids to tell about powerful miracles they've learned from the Bible or experienced in their lives. Close with sentence prayers: **Lord, thank you for showing your power in . . .**

EXTRA MILE IDEA

Royalty Says

If possible, meet someplace—such as a mansion, a castle, a fancy room at a nearby university, or an ornate government building—that will remind children of royalty. Before the meeting, make a "scepter" by putting a wrapping-paper bow on the end of a wooden or metal rod.

Have kids sit on the floor in a circle. Play music and have kids pass the scepter around the circle until the music stops. Explain that whoever is holding the scepter when the music stops becomes king or queen for that round. As in Simon Says, the king or queen gives a command—such as "Stand on one foot" or "Cluck like a chicken"—that the rest of the group must follow. Continue the game until everyone has had a chance to be king or queen. Afterward, ask:

● **What was the best part about being king or queen?**
● **What would it be like to be king or queen of the whole earth?**
● **What do you think the king or queen of the whole earth could do?**

Read aloud Psalm 47:1-2, 8-9. Say: **As the Bible says, God is king over all the earth. In the same way that you had control when you were king or queen, God has control all the time. He is the most powerful person in the whole world because he is king of the whole earth.**

Have kids stand up, bow to the King, and sing a favorite praise song.

Chapter Three

Our Creator God

In many public school science classes, there is no such thing as a personal Creator. God is replaced by human reason and the scientific method. In other words, those who have placed their faith in science seek to erase a key element of the Judeo-Christian faith: belief in the God of Creation. With children from unchurched homes, they just might succeed.

That's why it's important to teach children that the God of the Bible, the God who created the heavens and the earth, is their God. They need to get to know the Creator better so they can withstand the pressure at school and in society not to believe in God at all. Use the ideas in this chapter to help children learn more about their Creator.

● ● ●

Cooperative Creation Mural

Form five teams. Assign each team one of the following passages: Psalm 104:1-4, 5-9, 10-18, 19-23, 24-28.

Provide paper, crayons, markers, scissors, and tape for everyone to use. Give kids 10 minutes to read and discuss their verses and make a drawing that communicates what those verses teach.

After 10 minutes, read Psalm 104:1-28 aloud while team members tape their pictures together to create a mural. Then ask:

- **Which team had the easiest part of the creation mural? Why?**
- **Which team had the hardest? Why?**
- **What is your favorite part of creation?**
- **Was creating this mural easy or hard for you?**

- Do you think creating the world was easy or hard for God?
- Do you think God is happy with creation now? Why or why not?
- How should we respond to God as the creator?

Say: **God created everything we see. God wants us to praise him for this wonderful creation.**

Creation Creatures

Read aloud Genesis 1:20-25. Form groups of five or six. Say: **As a group, choose a creature from God's creation to pantomime. The rest of the groups will guess which animal you're pantomiming. Your group will pantomime only one animal, and each person in your group will be a part of that animal. For example, if your group chooses a snake, four of you could be the body, one the head, and one the tongue that darts out of the snake's mouth. You may use props from this room, but make sure your animal doesn't make a sound.**

Check to make sure each group chooses a different animal. Have kids applaud each group after its pantomime. Then have everyone sit down. Ask:

- **Why did God create different animals?**

Talk about the value to the earth of each animal pantomimed. For example, cows give milk and meat, lizards eat bugs, and peacocks offer great beauty.

Say: **God is a very wise creator who created all animals for a purpose. He specially designed each of them for his own enjoyment.**

Creation Scramble

Before class, write the names or tape pictures of things in God's creation on 3×5 cards. For instance, you might write "river" on one card and tape a picture of a zebra on another.

Say: **I'm going to attach to your back a picture or name of something God has created. Each of you has the job of figuring out what's on your back by asking others yes or no questions. For example, you might want to ask: Does it breathe? Does it walk? Can you eat it? Is it on land? Once you've discovered what's on your back, sit down in a circle.**

Once kids are seated, say: **Listen to what God's Word says about God's role in creation.** Read aloud Psalm 65:9-13. Then ask:

- Why do you think God created these things?
- Is God still creating things today? Explain.
- How does God take care of the earth?
- Does our world look the same today as it did when God first created it? Why or why not?
- What would you say to help someone believe that God created everything?

Say: **God created the earth, but he didn't leave it alone. God is still taking care of all the things he created.**

Creative Creator

Arrange ahead of time to take your group to a petting zoo or farm.

After arriving at your destination, form trios. Give each trio a 3×5 card and a pencil. Instruct kids to observe the animals, choose one animal, and write ways that animal is different from other animals. For example, a giraffe has a long neck, and a duck has webbed feet.

After 20 minutes, gather everyone and have trios each report their observations to the rest of the group. Then read aloud Genesis 1:20-26. Ask:

- Why do you think God created animals?
- Why do you think God created people?
- Why do you think God made every animal different from all the others and every person different from every other person?
- What do God's creations tell you about the kind of creator God is?

Say: **God is a creative God. We can learn more about the colors, shapes, and textures God likes when we observe his handiwork. Seeing what God has made can help us learn more about what God is like.**

Creative Wonders

Form trios. Give each trio a sheet of paper that's been folded into thirds and a pencil.

Have trio members sit with their backs to each other. Have one member draw a face and neck on the top third of the paper, fold the paper so that the picture can't be seen, then pass the paper to the next artist. The second artist should draw the arms and torso on the middle third of the paper, fold the paper so only the bottom third is visible, and pass it to the third artist. Have the third artist draw the legs and feet.

Say: **Unfold your paper to see the results of your team's artistic efforts.**

Have the group vote on the silliest, scariest, and most lifelike creatures. Then read aloud Psalm 139:13-14. Ask:

● **How is the way God made us different from the way we made our creations?**

● **What does it mean that God made our whole beings?**

● **What are some examples of how we are made in "amazing and wonderful" ways?**

Say: **Aren't you glad God was in charge of creating us? If he hadn't had a plan, we could've turned out like these crazy pictures we drew!**

Every Color Under Heaven

Form three groups. Say each of the following phrases from Psalm 104, having each group complete its assignment before you move on to the next phrase.

● **Lord, you have made many things.** Have group 1 say a number between one and five.

● **With your wisdom you made them all.** Give group 2 a container of M&M's and Skittles. Have them shake out the number of candies equal to group 1's choice.

● **The earth is full of your riches.** Tell group 3 they have 15 seconds to name things in God's creation. The things they name must correspond to the colors of the candies, and they must name as many things of each color as the number chosen by group 1.

For example, if group 1 chooses the number two and group 2 shakes out red and yellow candies, group 3 will have to name two red things in God's creation, such as a flower and a ladybug, and two yellow things, such as the sun and a lemon.

After each round, rotate the groups' responsibilities. After each group has had several turns, share the remaining candy with everyone. Say: **You've just listed many things that God created.** Then ask:

● **How do things God created meet people's needs?**

● **Do you think people are taking good care of God's creation? Why or why not?**

● **If God put you in charge of his creation, what would you do?**

Say: **God has put each of us in charge of his creation. God wants us to take care of what he has created.**

Exploding Dictionary

Form teams and have each team sit at a table. Pass out old newspapers and tell teams to cut out individual letters from a newspaper and drop the letters into a paper grocery sack. Say: **The more letters your team cuts out, the better chance your team has of winning the game!**

After two or three minutes, have members of each team shake their sack vigorously. Say: **Spill your sack onto the table. The team that has a dictionary fall on the table is the winner.**

Kids will think you're crazy, but have them do this anyway. Ask:

● **Why didn't a dictionary fall out?**

● **Some people believe that the world came into being in a similar way, that there was a huge explosion and everything just fell into place without any help from God. What do you think of this theory?**

Read aloud John 1:1-3. Have kids each arrange the letters to spell their names.

Say: **Just as a dictionary didn't fall out of your paper sack, the world didn't just happen to create itself. Just as you had to put your letters in order, God put the world in order. God is the creative mind behind creation.**

Globe Glob

Have kids stand in a circle. Stand in the center of the circle as you describe this activity. Pretend to hold "Globe Glob" while you talk.

Say: **I'm holding in my hands a very special substance used to create things. It's called Globe Glob. You can't see it, but it's here. I'm going to give you some Globe Glob and have you create anything you want to. You can't talk as you create. As you work, your Globe Glob can be anything you want it to be—gooey or hard like metal. Think of something you want to create, and I'll come around and give you some Globe Glob.**

As you "distribute" the Globe Glob, say: **You might create an airplane, hop in it, and fly around the room. Or you might create something that has never been created before.**

After two minutes, bring kids back together to describe and demonstrate their creations.

Read 2 Peter 3:13. Then ask:

● **What does this verse tell us about what God is doing?**

● **What do you think this new heaven and new earth will look like?**

● What do you hope will be in this new heaven? this new earth?

Say: **God created this wonderful earth that we live on. And he will create a new heaven and earth for his children to live in. Let's thank God for providing these places for us.**

Close in prayer.

In His Image

Give each of the children three pipe cleaners. Say: **It's fun to make things. Let's be creative and make these things.**

Instruct each child to make a different "impossible" creation such as a sunset, a thunderstorm, a field full of wildflowers, or a world.

When the children protest that they can't make these things, say: **That's right. These are just a few of the wonderful things God has created. The Bible tells us about some of the things God created.**

Read aloud Genesis 1:26-27. Ask:

● **What does it mean to be created in the image of God?**

● **If being in God's image means being like God, how are we like God?**

Say: **You may not be able to create all the grand things God has, but God has made you creative. Use your pipe cleaners to create a model of something you're thankful God made. For example, you may want to make your pipe cleaners look like a flower, the sun, or a person.**

Once kids' creations are finished, lead them in thanking God for the things he has made.

Rainbow Rock Gardens

Assist kids in making these crystal gardens. Give each child a pie tin. Have children arrange sticks, stones, and charcoal briquettes in their pie tins.

Move a safe distance away from the children and mix together 6 tablespoons salt, 6 tablespoons bluing (found in the laundry section at many grocery stores), 6 tablespoons water, and 1 tablespoon ammonia. (Caution: Avoid inhaling ammonia fumes and keep the crystal gardens and ammonia out of reach of small children.)

Pour a bit of the mixture over each child's rock garden. Next, have children squeeze drops of food coloring on the rock gardens. Every 20 or 30 minutes, have children check their gardens.

Read aloud Genesis 1:1. Say: **We used a recipe to create something.** Ask:

● **Do you think God used a recipe to create the world?**

● **Did God have ingredients, or did he create everything out of nothing?**

Help kids slip the pie tins into plastic grocery bags to carry them home safely. Then say: **Take your crystal garden home and watch it grow. Your crystal garden should continue to grow and look attractive for at least a week. As you watch what we've created, remember that God created our world. He created something out of nothing.**

Wonderfully Made

Play Follow the Leader three times with a different leader each time. Have the first leader name actions to be followed and do them at the same time. Have the second leader mime the actions but not say anything. Then blindfold the kids. Have the third leader name actions, which the kids should try to do without seeing. Have each leader lead for two or three minutes.

Remove the blindfolds from the kids and ask:

● **When was it hardest to follow the leader? When was it easiest?**

● **What parts of your body were most helpful in this game?**

● **Who made it possible for your body to move the way it does?**

● **In how many different places can you bend your arms? your hands?**

After kids have responded, say: **Listen to what King David said about his body in the Bible.** Read aloud Psalm 139:15-16.

Say: **Imagine what it would be like if our bodies were made differently.** Ask:

● **What are some silly variations of the way we're made?**

● **What if your arms and hands didn't bend?**

● **What if your feet faced the other way?**

● **What if you had ears for a nose?**

Say: **We've gotten used to the way we look, but I think God was very wise in designing us this way. Let's thank God for making us wonderful.**

Close in prayer.

Cookie Creations

Provide animal crackers or small gingerbread or sugar cookies in the shapes of animals, people, stars, trees, or fish. Have kids paint two of three coats of clear fingernail polish or tempera paint and varnish over the food. Then have them glue a pin backing to the back of each creation.

Read aloud Genesis 1:12 and Acts 17:24. Then ask:

● **Out of all the things God created, what would you miss if God hadn't made it?**

● **What's your favorite creation? Why?**

● **If you could ask God any question about his creation, what would you ask?**

● **What do you think God's answer would be?**

Say: **You can't eat these cookie creations, but you can wear them home to remind you that God created everything.**

Chapter Four

Our All-Knowing God

The fact that our God knows everything is comforting and frightening at the same time. If God knows everything, then he knows when I'm sad, struggling, or in danger. But if God knows everything, then he also knows what I'm thinking when I'm angry, what I do in secret, and who I really am.

 Children need to understand both aspects of our all-knowing God. As they get to know God better, they'll also understand that God is both a holy God who hates sin and a loving God who is quick to forgive. Getting to know our omniscient God will give children a greater accountability to God, a greater capacity to please God, and a greater appreciation for God's instructions for life. Use this chapter to introduce children to our God who knows all.

● ● ●

Come Find Me, God

Say: **I'd like you to help me find someplace where we can hide from God. We're going to start our search here at the church. Please take off your shoes and socks so we can quietly find a place to hide.**

You may want to have dark glasses or other disguises for the children to wear. As a leader, you must be very convincing that you believe there's a place to hide from God.

Take the group throughout the church on a hunt to find the best place to hide from God. Try under the church pews or in the custodian's closet. Take children into a corner of the church office, a furnace room, or any other out-of-the-way place. At each place you stop and hide, say: **I think this is a good place to hide from God, don't you?**

Do you think God can see us?

Wait for kids' responses each time. Then say: **Even if this isn't a good place, I'm sure we'll find one! Let's go find a new hiding place.**

During your hunt, children may come up with the correct answer—that there's no place to hide from God. Continue to assure them that you can find a place. They'll become more confident that there's nowhere to hide each time you stop. And they'll love knowing the answer before you do!

When you've run out of hiding places, sit down with the group, act frustrated, and say: **Well, we didn't find a good hiding place here at church, but this is God's house. Can you think of somewhere else we could hide, maybe in your home? school? outside? Well, let's see what God's Word has to say about hiding.**

Read aloud Psalm 139:7-12. Act amazed!

Say: **Why, you were right! There is no place that we can hide from God! He knows everything.** Ask:

● **Do you think that sometimes we try to hide things from God, even when we know he knows everything about us?**

● **What is something people might want to hide from God? Explain.**

● **Does God want us to try to hide things from him? Why or why not?**

● **What does God want us to do instead of trying to hide things from him?**

Say: **God doesn't want us to try to hide from him. God loves us and knows everything about us. God wants us to be honest and not sneaky with him.**

Face Off

You'll need a self-stick note for each child. Before class, write the words "sad" or "happy" on each note. You'll need an equal number of sad and happy notes.

Give each child one of the notes and a large paper sack. Say: **Don't let anyone see your label. As soon as you read your label, stick it to your forehead, put the paper sack over your head, and make the face on your label.**

After all the children's faces are covered, touch a child's shoulder and guess which face the child is making. Then have the child take off his or her sack. Have that child help you guess which expression is on the next face. Continue until every sack has been removed.

Say: **Listen to what the Bible says about what God knows.**

Read aloud Psalm 94:11. Ask:

● **Did you know which facial expression you'd find under the sack?**

● **Did God know which facial expression was under the sack? Why or why not?**

● **How does it make you feel to know that God knows your thoughts?**

Say: **God knows all of your thoughts. He knows when you're happy or sad. God knows everything about you and loves you all the time.**

Guess, Please

Form teams of up to five children each. Give each team a paper sack with different objects inside. Be sure sacks are securely stapled shut. Direct each team to select one person to record guesses. Then have other team members each take a turn guessing what items are in the sacks (no peeking!). After everyone has had a chance to guess, reveal the contents of the sacks, comparing kids' recorded guesses with the actual items in the sacks. Ask:

● **How did you do at guessing what was in your sack?**

● **What would've made it easier to guess?**

Say: **Listen to a story from the Bible that tells what Jesus knew about one of his disciples.**

Read aloud John 1:43-51. Ask:

● **Do you think Jesus was just guessing about Nathanael? Why or why not?**

● **What does God know about you?**

● **Is there anything God doesn't know about you? Explain.**

● **Are you glad God knows everything about you? Why or why not?**

Say: **God knows everything about you—what you had for breakfast, what you're thinking about right now, what you dream about being when you grow up. And God loves you—even when you might do things that aren't very nice. God loves you all the time.**

Hide and Seek

Play a mental form of Hide and Seek. Form pairs and have partners take turns "hiding" in the room by thinking of a hiding place. In this game, they can fit into the tiniest of places! Have their partners guess the hiding place while the "hidden" children tell them if they are getting warmer or colder. When everyone has had a chance to hide, end the game. Then ask:

● Who hid in the most unusual place?
● Did it take a long time to find you? Why or why not?

Read aloud Acts 5:1-11. (Consider carefully whether to use this story with younger children. You could also use Psalm 139:1-4 as the Scripture to explore.) If you use Acts 5:1-11, ask:

● Did Ananias and Sapphira think they could hide their thoughts from God? Why or why not?
● How did the Holy Spirit know what they were thinking?
● What would happen if this happened to people every time they lied?
● Are there times you try to hide your thoughts from God?

Say: God is not going to strike you dead if you lie, but you will experience a break in your relationship with God until you admit to God that you sinned. God knows everything you do.

I Never Knew

One week prior to using this activity, have kids find out from their parents or grandparents one story or fact about themselves that they didn't previously know. Have them bring that story to the next meeting.

Have kids sit in a circle and tell their stories. Afterward, read aloud Matthew 26:31-35, 69-75. Ask:

● How did Jesus know what Peter would do?
● Does Jesus know what you'll do tonight? tomorrow? 10 years from now?
● Does anyone know you better than God? Explain.

Say: Just as your parents and grandparents know you well, Jesus knows you well. Your parents and grandparents know a lot of things about you that no one else knows. However, Jesus knows everything about you—even more than your parents and grandparents.

Inside Out

Say: The Bible tells us about what God knows. Listen to these verses from the book of Job. Read aloud Job 38:1-12.

Give each child a sheet of paper. Have each child draw one thing mentioned in the Bible passage that God knows about. Then give each child a piece of tape and have children tape their pictures to a wall.

Turn off the lights. Turn on a flashlight and hand it to a child. Using a second flashlight to help you see, reread the passage. As you read, have kids pass the flashlight down the row and shine it on their pictures. After the reading, ask:

● **What does this passage say that God knows about the world?**

● **What are things God knows that we haven't mentioned or that aren't pictured on our wall?**

● **Does God know everything? Explain.**

● **How will knowing that God knows everything about you affect the way you think and act?**

Say: **God knows everything about you. When you're in trouble, God knows. When you sin, God knows. We can trust God to help us because he always knows what we're going through.**

Plans for You

Give children pencils and identical sheets of white paper. Have children trace around their left hands on their papers. Then have them write their names lightly on the back of their papers. Collect the papers and mix them up. Then hold up the papers one at a time and have children guess which hand print is theirs.

Say: **Many of you recognized your hand print by some special mark. God not only knows every part of you—including that special mark—he also has special plans for the way he created you. Listen to God's plan for you.**

Read aloud Jeremiah 29:11. Ask:

● **What does Jeremiah 29:11 mean to you?**

● **How does this make you feel about God?**

Say: **God knows your hand print and everything about you. God knows your future, too. He has very special plans for you.**

Secrets

Have each child use these questions to interview three other children:

● Do you have a secret you can tell me so that I can know what you know?

● What is there that you don't know but would like to know?

After 10 minutes, bring all the children together to report their interviews. Then ask:

● **What was the most interesting thing you learned in your interviews?**

● **How did you feel when you were asked to tell a secret?**

● **What are some of the things most people wish they knew about?**

● **Does anyone know everything there is to know?**

● **Is there anyone else who can or will know everything about everything?**

Say: **Listen to what the Bible says about someone who knows everything.**

Read aloud Deuteronomy 29:29. Ask:

● **What are some things that only God knows?**

● **How do you feel about God knowing these things but not telling us?**

● **Why does God keep some things secret from us?**

Say: **God knows everything, and there are some things that God tells us and some that God doesn't. These things are a mystery to us. In his wisdom, God reveals these things to us in his time.**

See It and Say It

While children are out of the room, partially hide an object, such as a small toy dog, somewhere in the room. When children return, tell them about the hidden object.

Say: **When you see the object, try to keep its hiding place a secret. Don't touch or stare at it. Only say, "I saw it and I said it!"**

Have children sit after they've discovered the hidden object. When the entire group is seated, say: **The Bible tells us about two people who tried to hide from God.**

Read aloud Genesis 3:1-13. Ask:

● **Why did Adam and Eve try to hide from God?**

● **Could they really hide from God? Why or why not?**

● **Did God already know what Adam and Eve had done? Explain.**

● **What does God want us to do when we do something wrong?**

Say: **When we do something wrong, our temptation is to hide from God because we think he is going to punish us. However, God**

wants us to come out of hiding and ask him for forgiveness.

Read aloud 1 John 1:9. Then direct children to pray silently and ask God's forgiveness for anything they've been trying to hide.

Something Fishy

Before class, fill a jar with goldfish-shaped crackers. Be sure to count the crackers as you put them in the jar. Have kids each guess the number of fish in the jar. List each child's name and his or her guess. Ask:

● **Do you think God knows the number of fish in the jar?**

Reveal the exact number and have the child who came the closest to the actual amount pass out a handful of crackers to each child. While the class is snacking, retell the story from Matthew 17:24-27. Ask:

● **What did Jesus know in this story?**

● **How could he have known that about the fish?**

● **Does God know everything about the world? Explain.**

Have each child create a fish out of construction paper, tissue paper, scissors, glue, a penny, and a paper clip. Instruct kids to cut out a fish shape from the construction paper. Show them how to cut out scale-like pieces of tissue paper and glue them to the fish's body. Then have children use the paper clip to connect the penny to the fish's mouth.

If time allows, put everyone's fish on the floor and have each child go fishing for his or her fish. Tie a magnet to the end of a string, then toss the magnet out to "hook" a fish. The magnet will attach to the paper clips, and kids can pull out their fish.

Say: **God provided for Peter's need with the coin in the fish's mouth. God knows your needs, and he will provide for you, too.**

Thinking of Something

Form groups of four and have kids number off within their groups. Tell kids that one child in each group will think of something while everyone else in the group tries to guess what it is. Read aloud the following statements so everyone knows the category the thinkers have been assigned. After you read each statement, allow time for each group member to guess once what the thinker is thinking.

● **Ones, think of a way to show love to a family member.**

● **Twos, think of something nice you can do for a neighbor.**

● **Threes, think of a way to honor a teacher.**

● Fours, think of something to do for a sick friend.

After everyone has had a chance to think of something, have kids form a circle and ask:

● Was it easy or difficult to guess what other people were thinking? Explain.

● Is it easy or difficult for God to know what we're thinking?

Read aloud Psalm 139:1-4. Say: **There is one person who knows our thoughts all the time. God knows everything. He knows all about us, and he knows all about everything around us.**

Go around the circle and ask children each to tell you one thing they don't know that they'd like to know. Then close with a prayer similar to this one:

Dear God, we have a lot of unanswered questions, but we're very glad that you have all the answers and will help us find the answers we need to know. Amen.

EXTRA MILE IDEA

Uniquely Me

As children arrive, have each use an ink pad to place a thumbprint on a sheet of poster board. Number in order the thumbprints on the poster board. On a separate sheet of paper, record which thumbprints belong to which child, but don't let kids see this.

Arrange for a police officer or some other expert to attend the meeting and talk about fingerprints. Have this person tell children about how each person's fingerprints are unique, how fingerprints are used to help police do their work, and how fingerprints can protect and help us.

After the talk, have children return to the poster board. Give each child a sheet of paper and a pencil. Have children write each person's name on the sheet of paper and list beside each name the number of the thumbprint that they think belongs to that person.

Afterward, reveal which thumbprints belong to which person. Then ask:

● Was it easy or difficult to match our thumbprints?

● Who made your thumbprints?

● Who knows all the thumbprints in the world?

Read aloud the first sentence of Jeremiah 12:3. Say: **It may be hard for us to match the thumbprints, but God knows everything about you. He created you. And he knows even what the lines on your thumbs look like. God knows you and loves you.**

Chapter Five

Our Ever-Present God

"**G**od is everywhere," some people in the New Age movement claim. "He is in you and me…in the trees…in the animals…God is everywhere."

This is not what Christians mean when we say that God is everywhere—and children need to understand the difference. God is not a force that permeates every living thing on earth. God is a personal being who knows no boundaries. Therefore, his presence is everywhere. However, God does not automatically live in every person. He wants us to respond to the love and grace he offers. Children need to  understand that this ever-present God waits longingly and patiently for the invitation to dwell in them.

Use this chapter to give comfort to children as they discover more about God's omnipresent power.

● ● ●

Buddy Up

Form pairs. Have partners perform tasks with their backs together and their arms linked. For example, have pairs sit in a chair, crawl under a table, put jelly beans in a jar, or give each other a drink.

Say: **Listen to what the Bible says about someone who is with you at all times.** Read aloud Hebrews 13:5 and Proverbs 15:3. Ask:

● **What was it like having your partner with you everywhere you went?**

● **Did you do things differently because your partner was with you? Explain.**

● **How was having your partner with you like God being with** you at all times? How was it different?

● How does having God with you at all times affect what you say or do?

Say: **God is just like a partner who is with us at all times. God has promised that he will never leave us.**

God-Is-Near Reminders

Form pairs. Have partners describe one time when they felt alone or frightened.

Say: **The Bible has some comfort for us when we are alone or frightened.** Read aloud Isaiah 43:1-5. Have partners discuss whether or not they felt God was with them when they felt alone or frightened. After discussion time, ask:

● **How did knowing that God was present make a difference at that time?**

● **How might things have been different if you had remembered God's presence?**

Have children make bracelets to wear as reminders of God's presence. Give each child three 12-inch pieces of different-colored yarn. As you distribute the first piece of yarn, say: **God, the Father.** Say: **God, the Son** as you hand out the second. Say: **God, the Holy Spirit** as you distribute the third.

Have children knot the pieces together about 2 inches from one end, braid the yarn together until there are approximately 2 inches left at the other, then knot that end.

Have partners tie on each other's bracelets as they say, "Do not be afraid—God is always with you!" Have children sit in a circle. Ask:

● **Why do you think God is always here for us?**

● **Is there anything we can do that would make God leave us?**

● **Does it help to know that God is with us when we are afraid?**

● **Who helps you remember that God is near?**

● **How can you help others remember?**

Encourage children to wear their bracelets as a reminder that God— the Father, the Son, and the Holy Spirit—is always present.

God's Port in a Storm

Form two teams. Have two members of each team stand aside as the rest of the team sits in the shape of a U. The opening of the U is the entrance to the "port." Have one person from each U stand in the opening and act as a lighthouse.

Blindfold the two team members from each team and say: **You are the ships. You're in the fog and can't see. The lighthouse will be here to guide you to port. The goal for your team is to have both ships make it safely into port. The lighthouse will be the only one who can make noise. To help give direction, the lighthouse can say "bleep, bleep" for the ship to go right and "bleep" for the ship to go left. If a ship should go straight ahead, the lighthouse can make a long, low "bleep." Those of you sitting in the U are the rocks. If a ship runs into you, it crashes and won't make it into port.**

Before the ships start to sail, spin them around several times so it's more difficult to make port. Give each child an opportunity to be a lighthouse or a ship. The team that gets the most ships into port wins. Afterward, ask:

● How did it feel to be a ship and unable to see?

● How helpful were the directions from the lighthouse?

● What was it like to trust someone for directions when you couldn't see that person? What was it like to be a lighthouse?

● How well did the ships respond when you gave directions?

Say: **Listen to what the Bible says about God's guiding presence.** Read aloud Joshua 1:9. Ask:

● How is God like a lighthouse for us?

● Can you think of a time you couldn't feel God with you?

● How do you know God is always with you?

● How can you know God is with you at school? at home? when you're lost?

Form pairs. Have partners pray for those areas in each other's lives in which they need to know God is with them.

Help Me

Take kids to a large open space (outside, if weather permits). Explain that they're going to play a game of Freeze Tag, but with a twist. Every time they tag and unfreeze someone, they automatically become frozen. Begin the game yourself by being "It."

As a result of the new rule, many will experience the feeling of needing help but being ignored. Others may experience the feeling of being helped at another's expense. Allow time for this to happen, then stop the game.

Form pairs. Have partners tell about times they were in trouble and needed help.

Say: **The Bible tells us that God helps us when we're in trouble.**

Then have children read Psalm 46:1-7. Read this passage aloud for younger children. Have partners discuss what they think the passage means. Ask:

● **How did you feel during this game?**

Say: **Think about times you were in trouble and needed help.** Ask:

● **What happened if no one helped you?**

● **What happened if you were helped?**

Say: **God is the only person who can be there to help us all the time. Though sometimes people don't know we need help or don't want to help us, God always knows when we need help and he always wants to help us. Let's thank God for times he's helped us.**

Close in prayer, having children each mention a time when God helped them as a prayer of thanks.

Hot Spot, Cold Spot

Bring a bag of small, individually wrapped candies to be a hidden treasure. You'll need at least one piece of candy for each child. Choose a child to be "It." Send It out of the room. Have the other players hide the candies all over the room. Then call It back to play.

Say: **Whenever** (It's name) **gets close to the hidden treasure, call "Hot spot!" Whenever** (It's name) **gets far away, call "Cold spot!" When It finds a candy, he or she gets to keep it. Then we'll choose a new It, retrieve the hidden candies, and repeat the game.**

Play the game several times. Then distribute candies to kids who haven't been It.

Say: **The Bible tells us about someone who is with us at all times.** Read aloud Isaiah 41:10. Ask:

● **Where is God?**

● **According to this verse, what does God do for us?**

● **How is that like what people did for us to help us find the candies? How is it different?**

● **How can having God with you at all times help you not to be afraid?**

● **What is something that scares you?**

As children each name a scary thing, have other children explain how God can be with them when those things scare them.

Say: **Let's pray and thank God for being with us at all times—even when we're afraid.** Close in prayer.

A Lock of Hair

Have the child with the longest hair sit in the front of the class. Hold a lock of the child's hair in your hand. Say: **Guess how many hairs are in my hand.**

Have each child come forward, touch the hair, and guess the number of hairs in the lock. Then have an adult count the number of hairs in the lock. Read aloud Matthew 10:29-31. Ask:

● **How many of you have counted all the hairs on your head?**
● **Do you notice when one of your hairs falls out?**
● **Why do you think God has counted all of our hairs?**

Say: **God always knows how many hairs we have, even when some have fallen out.** Ask:

● **If God keeps track of our hair, how often is he around us?**
● **How valuable does God say we are to him?**
● **How does God take care of us every day?**

Say: **God is always with us and always cares for us. Let's thank God for his constant care.** Close in prayer.

Model Christians

You'll need small resealable bags labeled "Jesus," larger resealable bags labeled "Father," 3×5-inch envelopes, 2×4-inch slips of paper with "Jesus" written on them, and permanent markers. Before class, write your name on one of the envelopes.

Say: **Today we're going to make a model of a Christian to remind us that God is always with us. Here's what the Bible says about God being with us.**

Read aloud John 14:18-21. Emphasize that Jesus is in us, we are in Jesus, and Jesus is in the Father. As you restate these three points, use the materials above to demonstrate the idea. Put the slip of paper with "Jesus" written on it into the envelope with your name written on it. Next, place the envelope inside the small bag labeled "Jesus." Then put the small bag inside the larger one labeled "Father" and seal the bag.

Have children make their own "Christians" to take home.

Encourage them to show others their models and to practice reciting John 14:20 as they do so.

My Shield

Form groups of four. Give each group a small blanket or towel. Have children work together in their groups to use their blankets to show something they can do in spring, summer, fall, and winter.

Read aloud Deuteronomy 33:26-29. Ask:

● **What does a blanket do for us? How is a blanket like a shield?**

● **What do these verses say God does for us?**

● **How is God like a blanket? How is he different?**

● **How does it make you feel to know that God shields you and goes to battle for you?**

● **Who does God battle?**

Say: **Just as a blanket can help us in every season, God is always helping us. He protects and shields us.**

Octopus Grab

In a large playing area, designate a player to be the "octopus." Tell the other children that they'll be "fish." Say: **The octopus is going to roam the ocean and catch fish. When the octopus shouts, "School's out!" all the fish must run through the playing area. When the octopus catches a fish, that fish turns into a helpful tentacle. The tentacles can run freely catching other fish until everyone is caught.**

After everyone has been caught, have the group sit in a circle. Say: **During this game, it seemed like the octopus was everywhere. Listen to where the Bible says God is.** Read aloud Isaiah 66:1-2. Ask:

● **Where is God? Where is a place that God isn't?**

● **How is God's presence like the octopus's presence in the game? How is it different?**

● **Do you think God is too big to bother with you? Why or why not?**

● **What do these verses say about who God is interested in?**

● **What does it mean not to be "proud or stubborn"?**

● **What does it mean to "fear God's Word"?**

● **How can we develop those characteristics?**

Say: **God is everywhere, helping his children. These verses tell us that God is especially interested in people who are not proud and** who love his Word.

Close in prayer, asking God to make you and the children these kind of people.

Sardines

Have children play this variation of Hide and Seek. Designate one child as "It." Have It hide while the other children cover their eyes. After five minutes, have all the children uncover their eyes and look for the hidden child. When someone discovers It, he or she shouldn't tell anyone. Instead, have that child quietly hide with It. Continue this process until all the children are packed like sardines in the secret hiding place.

After several rounds of play, say: **Let's find out from God's Word if we can hide from God.** Read aloud Psalm 139:7-12. Then ask:

● **Is it possible to hide from God?**

● **Where could you go that God would not be with you?**

● **How does knowing that God is always with you make you feel?**

Say: **Having faith in God is much like this game. We may try to hide from God, but we can't. When we try to hide, God goes right along with us and hides with us, too. God is always with us.**

Who's Watching

Write each child's name on a slip of paper. Fold these and have children each draw a name, returning slips only if they get their own names. Have children slowly walk around the room, randomly moving in any direction. Have each child watch the person whose name he or she chose. They should keep that child within sight at all times but not let the other child know who's watching. The object of the game is to discover who's watching you without letting that child know he or she has been discovered and without letting your own person out of sight.

After three minutes, have kids guess who was watching them. Then have the children tell who they were watching. Ask:

● **How did you feel about being constantly watched by someone?**

● **Which was more difficult: watching without being noticed or discovering who was watching you? Explain.**

Say: **Listen to what the Bible says about God.**

Read aloud Jeremiah 32:17-19. Ask:

- Why does God constantly watch us?
- How do you feel about having God watch you constantly?
- How can God watch everyone in the entire world at the same time?
- How do people sometimes try to get God to quit watching them?

Have kids sit with their arms around their knees and heads bowed, as though hiding. Pray: **God, sometimes we hide from you because we're afraid for you to know things about us.**

Say: **Think of the last thing you tried to hide from God and talk silently to God about it.**

Have kids raise their heads and open up their arms when they are finished. Pray: **God, thank you for being with us, for knowing everything about us, and for loving us even when we try to hide.**

EXTRA MILE IDEA

Look, I See Four!

Take your kids to a place where they can experience a fire. For example, you might take them to a bonfire or to a house with a fireplace. As kids gaze at the fire, read Daniel 3 from an easy-to-understand translation of the Bible.

After the story, give each child a piece of orange or yellow tissue paper. Have children draw pictures of times they knew God was helping them. Then have them each color a black body-silhouette as a reminder of how God took care of the men in the furnace and how he will take care of them.

Afterward, have children show their pictures and tell their stories. Then ask:

- **How do you think Shadrach, Meshach, and Abednego felt when the angel was with them in the fire?**
- **How would you have felt?**
- **How can we know that God is with us if we can't see him?**
- **Who can you tell your "fiery furnace" story to this week to help them know God better?**

Form pairs. Have partners share their pictures and stories and close in prayer, thanking God for being with them all the time.

Chapter Six

Our Loving God

If there is one attribute of God that children need to know, it is that God is love. In many ways, this is the most important characteristic to grasp because it gives meaning to everything else that God is. When we understand that God is not only all-powerful but also completely loving, we don't fear what he might do to us. And though we recognize that God is a holy God who hates our sin, we rely on his loving character to keep him from destroying us.

The fact that God is a loving God propels and gives meaning to our entire Christian faith. It was a loving God who sent Jesus to die for our sins, and it is a loving God who reaches out to children, inviting them to know him. Use this chapter to reinforce the truth that God is a loving God.

●●●

Can't Blow It Out

You'll need a trick candle. You can find trick candles in the birthday candle section of most grocery or variety stores.

Say: **Think of one thing you could do that might make God stop loving you. After I light the candle, say that thing, then blow out this candle.** Light the candle and say: **This is God's love.**

Then have children say the things they've thought of and try to blow out the candle. (If you have a large class, do this in groups of four to save time.) Afterward, ask:

● **What happened when you tried to blow out this candle?**
● **How is this candle like God's love for you? How is it different?**

47

● Can you ever make God stop loving you?

Say: **Listen to what God says will separate you from his love.** Read aloud Romans 8:37-39.

Say: **God will love us no matter what we do. Doesn't that make you feel great? Since God loves us so much, we should always try our hardest to be the kind of people he would like us to be. But it's great to know that even if we mess up, God will still love us.**

Clear Evidence

Arrange the meeting room ahead of time so that it resembles a courtroom. Place chairs on one side for witnesses and a chair in the center for the judge. The bailiff should stand by a chalkboard or an easel with newsprint on it. Decide beforehand who will be the judge and who will be the bailiff. Have the rest of the children be witnesses. (It's OK to have just one witness.)

Explain each role as follows: The witnesses must think of the one person (besides God) who loves them the most. The judge will ask the witnesses one at a time what evidence they have that the person they chose loves them the most. As each witness responds, the bailiff is to record the evidence on the chalkboard or newsprint.

After all witnesses have responded, prompt the judge to declare that everyone is loved the most—because they are each loved by God.

After acting out this "trial," form groups of three. Give each group a sheet of poster board and markers. Say: **The Bible gives us evidence that God loves us.**

Have each group read aloud Romans 5:6-8 and draw a picture that shows what these verses teach. (Read the verses aloud for younger children.) Once their pictures are drawn, bring everyone together. Ask:

● **What evidence do we have that God loves us?**

● **How does it make you feel to know that Jesus died for you?**

Referring to the list of evidence on the chalkboard or newsprint, ask:

● **Would any of these people die for you? Why or why not?**

● Would you die for anyone? Why or why not?

Say: **We've seen a lot of proof of people's love for us. But the Bible says that God proved his love for us even when we did not love him, in fact, when we hated him. God is a God of love who loves us even when we don't love him.**

Coin Hunt

Before class, hide a coin in your room. You will also need to bring rewards, such as small candies, for the teams that find the coin and hunt the best.

Form teams of three. Say: **There's a coin that's very valuable to our lesson lost in this room. I'm hoping that one of the teams can find it. On "go," hunt for it. There will be a reward for the team that finds the coin. There will also be a reward for the team that hunts the best. I will be watching for the teams that don't give up, so look hard for the coin. OK, go!**

After the coin has been found and the rewards given, say: **A woman in the Bible also lost a coin and searched for it.**

Read aloud Luke 15:8-10. Ask:

● **What does this parable say about how the woman hunted for the coin?**

● **How did you hunt for the coin today?**

● **How do you think God would hunt for us if we were lost?**

● **What does this say about how much God loves us?**

● **What are some other ways God has shown us he loves us?**

● **Who are the people in your life who remind you that God loves you?**

● **Where else can you go to be reminded that God loves you?**

Give everyone a piece of candy. As you hand the candy to each child, say: (Name of child), **God loves you!**

Great Is His Love

Before class, use a permanent marker to draw smiling faces on room temperature green grapes. Make enough for everyone in the class. Also, draw angry faces on about 12 grapes. During class, give each child a smiling grape and a sheet of white construction paper. Tell kids that the grapes are children they're responsible for. Have kids draw on the construction paper everything their children will need to have loving, healthy lives. After kids show and describe their drawings, have them sit in a half-circle.

Then say: **Listen to what God's Word says about how God takes care of us.**

Read aloud 1 John 3:1. Say: **Loving and caring for someone takes effort on our part. God takes care of us because he's our heavenly Father and he loves us.**

Display the "angry" grapes on the table. Explain that they represent the angry people who crucified Jesus. If possible, put a cross in the middle of the grapes.

Say: **Suppose you had to give your child to this angry crowd of people to die on a cross.** Ask:

● **Would you? Why or why not?**

Say: **That's what God did for us. He gave us his Son, Jesus.**

Read aloud 1 John 4:7-10. Each time the word "love" or "God" is mentioned in these verses, have the children stand then quickly sit down again. Read the passage aloud two or three times to emphasize how often these words are used.

Close with a prayer, thanking God for his love in sending Jesus, his greatest gift of all.

Love Hug

Say: **I'm going to read a passage from the Bible. Every time you hear the word "love," hug someone.** Read aloud 1 John 4:7-21.

Afterward, have children sit in a circle. Pass around a big red heart. Say: **Whoever has the heart when the lights flash, turn to the person on your right and say, "God loves you." Then hand the heart to that person.**

Continue this game until everyone has had a turn. Ask:

● **How did you feel when you got hugged? when you got the heart?**

● **How did you feel hugging someone? giving the heart to someone?**

● **Why do you think its important to show love to others?**

● **What makes you feel loved?**

Read aloud John 3:16. Ask:

● **Do you think it was easy for God to give up his Son for us? Explain.**

● **Why did God let his only Son die?**

● **Why does God want everyone in the world to believe in Jesus?**

● **How can you be involved in telling others about Jesus?**

Have kids each name one person they can tell about Jesus' love. Then close in prayer.

Love in Action

Give each child 10 paper hearts to use as coupons. Have children write on each heart one thing they can do to show love to others. For example, kids may write "clean someone's room" or "listen to some-one."

Say: **These heart coupons are a way you can show love to each other.**

Have children blindfold each other. Then space the children around the room three to four feet from each other.

Say: **Love is an action. We'll look for love by slowly walking around and gently bumping each other. Whoever bumps into someone will give one of his or her hearts to the person being bumped. If two or more people bump each other at the same time, they can exchange hearts. Let's see who has the most hearts at the end of this game.**

After the game, say: **The Bible encourages us to give love away.**

Read aloud Colossians 3:12-14. Then ask:

● How did it feel to give away your hearts? to get hearts?
● How does it feel to give away love? to get love?
● When was the last time you showed God's love to someone?
● How did that person respond?

Say: **Take your hearts home and use them as a reminder to show love to the people around you this week.**

Loved the Best

Form teams of four and direct one team to each corner of the room. Give each team four 3×5 cards and instruct them to write a different letter of the word "love" on each card. After teams lay their cards on the floor so they spell "love," have them each stand in a line five feet away from their cards. Give each team a penny to toss at their letters.

On "go," members of each team are to work together to land their penny on each card consecutively to spell out "love." The first team to spell out "love" is the winner.

After you have a winner, say: **The team that was the quickest is certainly the team that God loves the best.** Ask:

● **Do you think this is true? Why or why not?**

Say: **Let's see what the Bible says about that.**

Read aloud Matthew 20:1-16. Ask:

● **Do you think what happened to the people in this parable was fair? Why or why not?**

● **How would you have felt if you had worked all day and received the same pay as the people who came at the end of the day?**

● How can God love us all equally—aren't some of us better Christians than others?

● If God loves everyone equally, can you do anything to make God love you any more than he already does?

Say: **God loves all of us no matter what we do, whether we win or lose, whether we're tall or short, whether we're young or old. God doesn't love you because of what you do. God loves you simply because you're you.**

Seeds of Love

Before class, photocopy and cut apart the "Blossoms of Love" handout (p. 56). Place the "seeds" in a Manila envelope.

Have each child pick a seed from the envelope and draw a picture on the seed (stick figures are fine!) of what he or she thinks would grow from that seed if it were planted in his or her life. When the children are finished, have them share with one or two others what their pictures represent.

Read aloud Ephesians 5:1-2. Then ask:

● **According to these verses, how did Christ show his love for us?**

● **How can we imitate that love in our relationships with others?**

● **What do we need to do to keep God's love growing in our lives?**

Create a bulletin board with the pictures. Cut a large flower pot, stems, leaves, and flower petals from construction paper. Use the children's pictures as the centers of the flowers. Title the display, "Let God's Love Bloom in Your Life!"

Stubborn Love

Find a volunteer by asking:

● **Who in this class can be as stubborn as a mule?**

Select that child and have him or her sit in a chair at the front of the class. Whisper into the volunteer's ear: **No matter what I or anyone else says or does, do not get up from this chair.**

Say: **Let's assume that our stubborn child has hurt feelings and really needs to forgive us for what has happened. What are ways we could make** (child's name) **come to us and forgive us?**

After children respond, suggest the following tactics and direct a different child to try each one:

● Command/Authority—Prompt someone to say, "(Child's name), I'm the boss. Forgive us because I said so."

● Physical Force—Have someone attempt to gently pull or push the child out of the chair.

● Deception/Trickery—Direct someone to warn, "That land shark under your chair is going to get you if you don't forgive."

● Reward/Bribery—Have someone say, "I'll give you $10 if you come tell us that you forgive us."

After all attempts fail, say: **The best way for this child to forgive us is simply for him** (or her) **to choose to do so out of love.**

Read aloud 1 John 4:8-11. Ask:

● **Why does God love us?**

● **Did anyone command God to love us? force God to love us? trick God into loving us? bribe God to love us?**

● **Why are you so lovable to God?**

● **Is everyone in the world lovable to God? Why or why not?**

Close in prayer, thanking God for his love.

Unbroken

Form groups of four. Give each group 10 wooden matches. As a safety precaution, wet the heads of the matches so they can't be lit. Have someone in each group try to break one match. Then have someone else try to break two matches. Have groups keep adding one match until they can no longer break the matches.

Read aloud Jeremiah 31:3. Ask:

● **Why did it get harder to break the matches as you added more?**

● **How is the strength of God's everlasting love like the strength of many matches? How is it different?**

● **How can you keep God from loving you?**

● **How is God's love different from people's love?**

Say: **We can never keep God from loving us. God says his love is everlasting no matter what we do. He will always love us. We can't break the strength of God's love for us.**

Unscrambled

Before class, prepare three different-colored sets of paper hearts. Write a different word from 1 John 4:19 on each heart. Hide the hearts in the room before the children arrive.

Form three teams. Assign each team a color that matches one of the sets of hearts hidden in the room. Have teams search for their hearts and, after they find them, arrange them on the floor to figure out the secret message. When team members discover the secret message, have them sit down beside their line of hearts.

After each team has figured out the verse, ask:

- **What does this verse mean?**
- **How did God first love us?**
- **How does God teach us how to love others?**
- **How is God's love different from some people's love?**
- **Who is someone you love because God loves you?**
- **What can you do to show that person that God is love?**

Have each team choose a person to love and a way to show that person God's love. For example, a team may choose to bake cookies for a neighbor.

EXTRA MILE IDEA

Papier-Mâché Faces

This activity will take two meetings. Before the first class, use the following recipe to make glue.

4 cups non-self-rising wheat flour

1 cup sugar

1 gallon warm water

1 quart cold water

½ teaspoon oil of cinnamon

1. Mix flour and sugar together in a large pan.

2. Add a portion of the warm water and stir. Continue adding warm water and stirring until you've created a smooth paste.

3. Slowly add the rest of the warm water.

4. Stir to break up any lumps, then boil the mixture.

5. Stir the boiling mixture constantly until it becomes thick and clear.

6. Thin the glue with cold water until it is the desired consistency.

7. Add ½ teaspoon oil of cinnamon if you're not planning to use the glue the day you make it. You may store this paste for a few days in a warm place if you add the oil of cinnamon.

Bring old newspapers, balloons, napkins, tissues, and your homemade glue to the first class.

Lead the children in a balloon-blowing contest and help them tie off their balloons. Show children how to tear the newspapers into long strips approximately 1 inch wide. Have children drag each newspaper strip through the glue. (If the paste is too thick, thin it with water.)

Show children how to cover their balloons with glue-covered strips of newspaper. The first layer of strips should run in one direction. Each additional layer should run in a different direction. Have children apply up to five layers of strips to their balloons.

While kids are adding their layers, crumple napkins and tissues into a separate bowl of glue to make a soft pulp.

Say: **You're in charge of molding a brand-new face. It can be any way you want it to be. There are no wrong ways to do it! While you work, think of a name for your face. Also, decide what your face's favorite song is and be able to tell us what its favorite food is.**

Have children use the pulp to mold noses, ears, and other facial features onto their balloons.

Set the faces in a prominent place and have each child tell his or her face's name, favorite song, and favorite food. Say: **God made each of us special, and we know that God doesn't make mistakes. He loves us just the way we are.**

Allow the faces to dry for one week.

Bring yarn, tempera or poster paints, and paintbrushes to your next meeting. Have kids decorate their faces with these supplies.

Later, have kids hold and display their faces. Have children vote for the most glamorous, silliest, or scariest face. Say: **Regardless of how we look on the outside, God loves what's on the inside of us.**

Read aloud Psalm 100:3. Close in prayer, thanking God for all the special children he has made. Name each child and a special characteristic of that child.

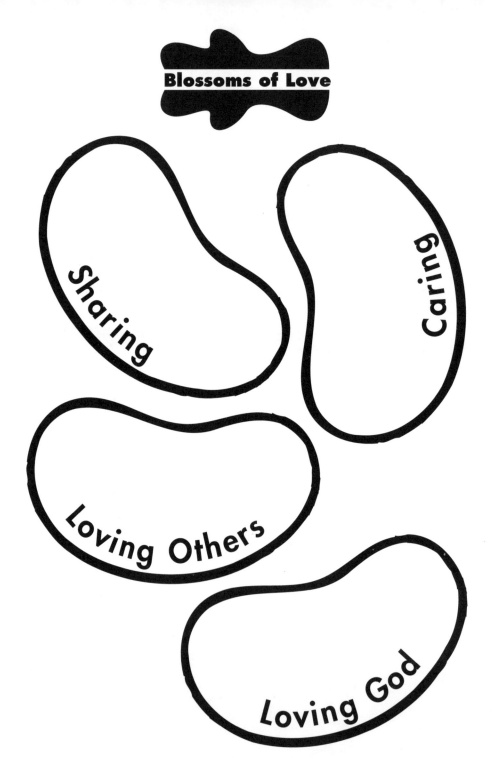

Blossoms of Love

Sharing

Caring

Loving Others

Loving God

Chapter Seven

Our Good God

"God is great, God is good, and we thank him for our food. Amen."

It's a simple prayer, a true prayer. But with it, perhaps we've done a disservice to our children. God *is* good, so let's celebrate! His goodness merits more than a solemn, singsong prayer.

In this chapter, you'll find ideas to help kids discover that God is good. God is their good shepherd who drops everything to search for them when they are lost. God also gives them good things to enjoy, simply because goodness flows from him. Finally, God's goodness is a purity that can also be called holiness. God is good! Use this chapter to help children understand how wonderful our God is.

● ● ●

Acrostic Prayer

Psalm 111 is an acrostic, which means that the lines of the psalm begin with successive letters of the Hebrew alphabet.

Have children read Psalm 111 aloud with you. Then ask:

● **What good things does God do for us?**
● **What gifts does God give us that we can't touch or see?**
● **How can we show God's goodness to others?**

Create a litany of thanks for the good things God does. Assign a letter of the alphabet to each person. Some children may need to have more than one letter. Have children think of good gifts from God that begin with the letters they have been assigned. For example, someone might say "apples" for A or "blessings" for B.

After children have listed their gifts, read aloud the following litany, having children name their gifts as indicated.

Leader: God of goodness, we thank you for (*items A, B, C, D, and E*). We praise your name.

Children: God is good! (*Raise arms high.*)

Leader: For (*items F, G, H, I, and J*), we praise your name.

Children: God is good! (*Raise arms high.*)

Leader: For (*items K, L, M, N, and O*), we praise your name.

Children: God is good! (*Raise arms high.*)

Leader: For (*items P, Q, R, S, and T*), we praise your name.

Children: God is good! (*Raise arms high.*)

Leader: For (*items U, V, W, X, Y, and Z*), we praise your name.

Children: God is good! (*Raise arms high.*) Amen!

Can't Touch This

Have children draw pictures of the items they consider to be their most prized possessions. Have children place their drawings in the center of the room. Then direct children to work together to decide which of the items pictured is the most important, the second in importance, and so on. Have kids make a single line of the items, beginning with the one they choose as the most important and ending with the item they consider the least important. Kids will probably disagree heatedly at times. If so, encourage them to move on to other items.

After five to 10 minutes (depending on the size of your group), bring kids together. Ask:

● **How do you feel about your item being placed where it is?**

● **What made this task so difficult?**

● **What makes something good and meaningful to us?**

Say: **Isaiah tells us in the Bible that God is to be highly valued and treasured even more than we value our prized possessions.**

Read aloud Isaiah 6:1-3. Ask:

● **What do you think it means to be "holy"?**

● **What do these verses tell us about God?**

● **Where would God be placed in this line? Explain.**

Say: **There are many people and things on this earth that are important and good. But not one person and not one thing is full of more goodness than God. After all, God is the one who created everything else that is good!**

Good Shepherd

Have children sit on the floor in a large circle. Say: **Today everyone gets a chance to be a shepherd.** Ask:

● **What's a shepherd?**
● **What makes a shepherd a good shepherd?**

Say: **The Bible tells us that Jesus is the good shepherd.**

Read aloud John 10:14-15. Say: **Jesus says, "I am the good shepherd." Let's see what it would be like to be a shepherd.**

Give each child a hook-shaped pipe cleaner for a shepherd's staff and a handful of cotton balls for sheep. Encourage children to count and name their sheep. Explain that they'll need to protect their sheep from dangers such as storms, wolves, and thorn bushes if they're going to be good shepherds.

After children have had time to count and name their sheep, use a blow-dryer to create a storm. Walk around the circle and try to blow the sheep away. The shepherds may use only their staffs to keep their sheep together. Next, reach around several students with a furry glove to represent a wolf trying to snatch sheep from their herds. Finally, drag a long strip of the fuzzy side of Velcro through the herds to snag a few sheep.

After these three attacks, ask:

● **What was it like trying to protect your sheep from the storm? the wolf? the thorn bush?**
● **What does Jesus protect you from?**
● **What do you think about Jesus always watching out for you?**

Say: **Jesus is the good shepherd. He loves us, and he protects us from harm.**

Good Things

Help kids arrange chairs in a circle and have everyone sit down. Start a rhythm by slapping your knees twice, then clapping your hands twice. Repeat the rhythm until everyone is doing it. Signal kids to continue the rhythm very quietly.

Say: **Making a rhythm is fun, isn't it? We can make rhythms like this because God gave us hands, legs, and a sense of timing. We're going to go around the circle and name other good things God has made. But we have to do it to the beat. OK? I'll start, then we'll go around to the right.**

As you continue the rhythm, say: **One good thing that God has made is hands.** Quickly gesture to the person on your right and help him or her name a good thing by repeating in rhythm: **One good thing that God has made is...** Continue until you've gone around the circle at least once. For fun, try doubling the speed the second time around the circle!

Say: **God has given us so many good things. Listen to what James 1:17 says.**

Read aloud James 1:17. Then ask:

● **What good things that God has made do you like best?**

● **Why do you think God gives us good things?**

Say: **God is good. He gives us good things because he loves us.**

Heavenly Taste-Test

Read aloud Psalm 34:1-8. Then read aloud verse 8a again: "Taste and see that the Lord is good" (NIV). Ask:

● **What does it mean to "taste" the Lord?**

● **How can you tell when something tastes good?**

● **How can you tell when something tastes bad?**

Give each child a piece of candy, chocolate, or fruit. As they eat, ask:

● **What makes this taste good?**

● **Why do you think the psalmist said that God tasted good?**

● **What has God done to show us that he is good?**

● **How is watching a sunset like tasting God's goodness?**

● **What about when someone we love gives us a hug?**

● **What are some other ways we can taste God's goodness?**

After everyone has shared, have kids give each other hugs as a demonstration of "tasting" God's goodness.

Never a Lie

Form groups of four to six. In this game, kids will tell one thing that is true and one that is not true in order to learn that God never lies.

Have group members each tell one thing they've really done and one thing they've never really done. After each child tells the two things, have the other group members vote on which is true and which is false. Afterward, ask:

● **Was it easy or difficult to tell when people were being truthful? when they were trying to fool us?**

● What do you think when someone lies to you on purpose?

● What do you think when you have a friend who is always honest?

Say: **Listen to what the Bible says about whether or not God can lie.**

Read aloud Numbers 23:19. Say: **The good thing about God is that we never have to guess if he is being truthful or not. The Bible says that he is always good and truthful.**

One Good Rap

Have kids form a circle and sing the first verse from "God Is So Good." After singing it through once or twice, tell kids you want them to turn the song into a rap. Demonstrate one way to do this by chanting the song lyrics and clapping between phrases to create a rhythm. For example, chant: **God is** (*clap*) **so good** (*clap, clap*). **God is** (*clap*) **so good** (*clap, clap*).

Form groups of six or fewer and have each group create its own rap version of the chorus. When everyone is ready, have groups present their raps. Applaud each group's efforts.

Afterward, read aloud Psalm 107:1. Have kids repeat the verse back to you three times. Then ask:

● **Why is it good to give thanks and praise to the Lord?**

● **Were you praising God's goodness when you presented your rap? Why or why not?**

● **How else can we praise God for his goodness?**

● **Can you think of any special ways God has been good to you?**

● **How can you praise him for the good things he has done for you?**

Form pairs and have partners praise God for the things he has done for them. Then close by chanting one or more of the kids' raps again.

Rainbows and Promises

Before class, cut out small rainbow shapes and hearts from construction paper.

Say: **Think of all the wonderful things God has given you. He has blessed you with many things and many people who love you. On each of these rainbows, draw a picture of something God has given you. You may use as many rainbows as you like. On each of these hearts, put the name of someone who loves you. You may use as many hearts as you wish.**

Help younger children write. When children have completed their rainbows and hearts, have them tape them to their clothing. Then have each child tell about his or her rainbows and hearts.

Say: **The Bible tells us about other ways God has shown his love for us.** Read aloud 1 Kings 8:54-56. Ask:

● **What does it mean to "bless" someone?**
● **Why did Solomon bless these people?**
● **Why does God want to bless you?**
● **How has God blessed you or made you happy?**

Say: **Solomon said that God keeps all his promises. God is good, so he never lies to us. Just as he placed a rainbow in the sky as a promise to Noah that he'd never again destroy the earth with a flood, God has promised to bless his children. Look at your hearts and rainbows and think about how God has done what he promised by giving you these blessings.**

Close in prayer, thanking God for all the blessings he has given the children.

Taste and See

Bring to class a jar of honey with a honeycomb in it and bread slices cut into strips. Ask:

● **What's one of your favorite foods that's also good for you?**
● **What's the sweetest food you like to eat?**

Say: **During Old Testament times, people didn't have lots of sweets like we do today. They didn't have candy or sugar like we use, but they did have honey. Honey was the sweetest food available, and it was a real treat.**

Show the jar of honey and the honeycomb. Point out that bees make the honey and store it in the honeycomb. Explain how the beekeeper opens the hive, removes the honeycomb, and drains out the honey for us to use. Give each child a strip of bread with a little honey on it. Tell kids not to eat the bread until you tell them to.

Say: **When David wrote Psalms 19 and 34, he remembered how good God is.**

Read aloud Psalms 19:9-10 and 34:8.

Instruct children to eat their bread and honey, then say together: **The Lord is good.** Have children name other things that help them know that God is good. After each person shares, lead the group in saying: **The Lord is good.**

Totally Pure

Before class, prepare three unmarked containers: one of peanut butter mixed with mustard, one of jelly mixed with pickle juice, and one of marshmallow creme. Prepare the first two so their original appearance isn't changed and kids won't know that there's a difference. You'll also need enough graham crackers for everyone in the group and plastic knives.

Form three groups and give each group one of the containers. Have each group choose a new and unusual name for its food and reasons someone would enjoy eating it. However, groups are not allowed to taste their own foods. Then have them prepare enough crackers for the other groups, present them to the groups, and explain why they are so good. After all three presentations are made, have everyone eat their snacks. Ask:

● **How did you respond when you were asked to eat something made by someone else?**

● **Which food seemed to be the pure version of what you were told it would be?**

● **How do you feel when you find out something is different from what you were told it would be?**

Say: **The Bible tells us that God will never trick us. He is always good.** Read aloud Deuteronomy 32:2-4. Ask:

● **How is God different from the yucky foods some of you just ate?**

● **What do these verses say God is like?**

● **According to these verses, why can we trust God?**

Say: **We can trust God not to trick us. God is always good and never changes.**

Ultimate Good

Read aloud 1 Corinthians 15:3-5. Have each child make a wooden cross from craft sticks. Give children colored sequins in the following order: gold, purple, red, white, and green. Have them glue the sequins to their crosses in the same order.

After kids finish their crosses, say: **The colors of the sequins on your cross mean something very special.**

The gold reminds us of God's home in heaven. God wants you to be with him in heaven someday.

But there's one thing that can never be in heaven—sin. The purple represents sin. Sin is anything that displeases God. God said that sin must be punished. The punishment for sin is death—to be separated from God forever.

The red tells us that God is good and wants to show his love for us. So God sent his Son, Jesus, to take the punishment for our sins. The blood Jesus shed is what enabled God to forgive us.

The white shows us that, when we accept what Jesus did for us, our sins are washed away and we're clean from sin.

Finally, the green tells us that there's new life with God and that we can grow to know him better each day.

Use your cross to remind you that God is good. God's goodness was shown when he let Jesus die on the cross so we could live with him in heaven forever.

EXTRA MILE IDEA

A Good Delivery

As a group, prepare a booklet based on Psalm 136:1-9 for a shut-in. Have each child choose and portray several verses from Psalm 136:1-9, then arrange all the finished pictures together in the sequence of the verses. Between each picture write the words, "For His lovingkindness is everlasting." Bind the pictures together in a folder or tie them together with yarn. Title your book "God's Lovingkindness." Make arrangements to deliver "God's Lovingkindness" together to your special person.

Chapter Eight

Our Wise God

Life can be pretty confusing when you're a kid. Parents tell you one thing, friends tell you another, and sometimes even the people at church tell you something different. Who really knows what's best for you? Who is the wisest person of all?

Children need to understand that God is the only one whose wisdom is infallible. God sees all and knows all. Learning that their God is all-wise will help children trust God more and seek God's guidance in making decisions. Through this process, the Bible will become more than a storybook to your children—they'll come to see it as the Word of God that guides them throughout life. Use this chapter to teach children that God is all-wise.

● ● ●

Crazy Definitions

Have fun with a game of Crazy Definitions. Bring a large dictionary to class. Open it at random and select a very unusual sounding word that most of the children won't know. Have children make up and tell crazy definitions for the word. After everyone has given a definition, read the correct definition. Repeat several times.

Hold up the dictionary and say: **It would be hard for anyone to know the definitions for all these words. But God knows them because God is wise. Listen to what the Bible says about God's wisdom.**

Read aloud Jeremiah 10:12. Ask:

● **What is something that God doesn't know?**

Say: **God knows all the facts. But God also knows how to use the facts so he does the right thing in every situation. That's what wis-**

dom means—knowing how to use knowledge in the best way. Ask:
- When do you need to know the right thing to do?
- Who do you talk to when you need wisdom?
- How can you get wisdom from God?

Remind children that God helps us by giving us wisdom, too. Pray and thank God for his wisdom. Then close by singing "God Is So Good" and substituting a new phrase, "God is so wise. He's so wise to me."

Deep Thoughts

Write the following hypothetical situations on 3×5 cards.
- Two sisters are in their bedroom. They're listening to their parents yell at each other as they always do. The little sister is crying. She asks, "Why do they always fight?" If you were the older sister, what would you say?
- The kids in the neighborhood are playing after school. They decide they don't want to play with your brother. They make fun of him, and he runs home to you. What do you tell him?
- You're the mother of a 12-year-old boy. Today, the principal called and said your son wasn't at school. You don't know where he was. When he comes home, you ask him how school went, and he says "fine." What do you do?

Form groups of four. Give each group a hypothetical situation. Give groups three or four minutes to discuss their situations and determine what they would do. Then have groups act out the situations and their responses to them.

After the groups have acted out their situations, ask:
- Why is it sometimes difficult to solve a problem?
- How do you feel when you face a problem and don't know how to solve it?

Say: Listen to what the Bible says about God's wisdom.

Read aloud Romans 11:33-36. Ask:
- What do these verses say about God?
- How do these verses make you feel about God?
- If you were facing a problem you couldn't solve, how could it help to know that God's wisdom is this deep?
- What is one problem that you'd like to ask God to help you with?

After kids tell their problems, lead them in prayer, asking God for wisdom in handling all the problems.

Do You Remember?

Before class, fill a large shoe box with an assortment of items such as a piece of candy, a peanut, an earring, a playing card, and a nickel. Put up to 20 items in the box, then place a lid on it.

Give each child a sheet of paper and a pencil. Take the lid off the box and have children look into it for one minute. Then cover the box and ask:

● **Can you remember what you saw?**

Instruct children to list everything they can remember. Then check the lists against the items in the box. Ask:

● **What helped you remember the things that you did remember?**

Say: **Listen to what God knows about you.**

Read aloud Matthew 10:29-31. Ask:

● **Can God remember the names of all the people on the earth? Why or why not?**

● **Does he know your name?**

● **What else does God know about you besides your name?**

● **How can God possibly keep track of how many hairs are on your head?**

Say: **God is all-wise. He knows and remembers everything about us. And he lovingly takes care of us.**

Guessing Game

Form groups of six and direct groups to sit in a circle. Have kids close their eyes. Give each group seven objects such as a crayon, a pencil, scissors, a spoon, a fork, a bottle of glue, and a paper clip. Have groups pass around the objects until they return to the first person in the circle. When the objects return to the first person, take them back. Then have the children guess what the objects were. Next, pass around the items while everyone's eyes are open. Ask:

● **How did you know what the items were?**

Say: **It would've been easier to identify the items if your eyes had been open. The Bible says that God is a light who opens our eyes.**

Read aloud 1 John 1:5. Ask:

● **What does it mean that God is light?**

● **How is not knowing something like being in the darkness?**

● **How can the light of God's wisdom help people when they're in darkness?**

Say: **God's light reveals the truth to us. As we live in God's light, we have his wisdom.**

Hot Seat

Set a chair in front of the class. Have children sit on the floor and face the chair. Say: **This is a Hot Seat. Whoever has wisdom can sit on this throne.**

Have the first volunteer sit on the Hot Seat. Lead the whole class in saying: **We salute you.**

Then, have the volunteer complete the following sentence, "I am the wisest person here because I can..." (Kids may name actions such as "dance," "swim," or "sing.")

Lead the class in shouting: **Show us!**

Have the volunteer show the action. Then have the volunteer say, "Who among you dares to challenge me?"

Have a second volunteer challenge the first by naming something he or she can do well, then sitting in the Hot Seat. Continue the process until everyone has sat in the Hot Seat.

Say: **Listen to what the Bible says makes us wise.**

Read aloud 1 Corinthians 1:25-29. Then ask:

● **Do the things we showed really make us wise? Why or why not?**
● **Can we find anyone in the world who is wiser than God?**
● **Why is God wiser than human beings?**
● **What is the best way to get wisdom from God?**
● **How can you use wisdom to honor God?**

Say: **God is the wisest of all. God gives us real wisdom if we ask for it.**

Hunt for Knowledge

Before class, make two sets of clues on two different colors of paper. Write the clues on small pieces of paper and hide them in the appropriate places around your meeting area (see page 69). Prepare a treat for the children to share at the end of the treasure hunt.

Form two teams. Have team members work together to figure out the clues, which are given in the form of riddles. If children can't yet read, read each clue as they find it. Begin the game by reading the first riddle.

RIDDLES

● **What has two arms, four legs, a back, but no head?** (Tape the copies of the next clue to the bottoms of chairs.)

● **When I am down, everybody is in the dark.** (Tape the copies of the next clue near light switches.)

● **You must go through me if you want to get anywhere.** (Tape the copies of the next clue in doorways.)

● **You're getting close. There's just one more clue. So why don't you stop and admire the view?** (Tape the copies of the next clue on windows.)

● **This is your last clue. The game's nearly over. But the treasure still remains under cover.** (Place the following note inside a Bible, marking Proverbs 2:1-8.)

● **You've won! Wisdom is your reward! Read Proverbs 2:1-8 to find out why your understanding is great!**

Give everyone a treat, then ask:

● **How did wisdom help you in this treasure hunt?**

● **Is wisdom different from just being smart? Explain.**

● **What's the difference between knowing something and understanding it?**

● **What makes God's wisdom greater than ours?**

● **What part does God's love play in God's wisdom?**

● **How are we to show our wisdom?**

Say: **God's wisdom is great. Just as you searched for treasure in this game, you can search for treasure and find it in God's Word.**

Life's a Puzzle

Give each person a piece from a puzzle containing at least 1,000 pieces. Tell each child to guess what the big picture of the puzzle is based on his or her puzzle piece.

After kids guess, let them put their puzzle pieces together and guess again what the big picture is. After everyone guesses, show kids the picture on the front of the puzzle box.

Say: **Listen to what the Bible says about how God looks at our life.** Read aloud Psalm 33:13-15. Ask:

● **How difficult was it to see the big picture of the puzzle?**

● **When God looks at your life, does he see the big picture or a puzzling set of small pieces?**

Say: **Though we may only see one piece at a time, God sees the big picture. Sometimes we don't understand why some things happen to us. But in time, God will help us trust that everything fits together to make our lives into a beautiful picture.**

Read aloud Psalm 33:20-22. Have kids hold up their puzzle pieces and think of puzzling or confusing things in their lives. For example, one child's parents may be getting a divorce, while another may have had to put a pet to sleep. As children think of these things, read aloud Psalm 33:20-22 as a prayer.

A Look at the Heart

Bring one uncooked and seven hard-boiled eggs to class.

Form eight groups and give each group markers and one egg to decorate to look like a king. Tell children that all the eggs are hard-boiled except one. (Don't tell them which egg is raw, but remember which group has the raw egg.)

Say: **Many times we concern ourselves with how we look on the outside and forget to think about what's in our hearts. Today, we'll see that God, in his wisdom, knows how important the inside is.**

Have kids form a circle, then paraphrase 1 Samuel 16:1-13, the story of David being chosen as king. Then say: **Show your "kingly" eggs and guess which one is David.**

Place a bowl in the middle of the circle. Have a person from each group use one hand to hold the group's egg over the bowl. Have a volunteer from the same group hit the egg firmly with a spoon handle to determine if it, indeed, is the chosen King David (the raw egg).

Provide wet paper towels to the person with the raw egg. Ask:

● How do we get to know the "inside" of others?

● Should we leave "looking on the inside" only to God?

● Why does it take God's wisdom to be able to see what people are really like on the inside?

Say: **God very wisely looks beyond what's on the outside of us and sees what's inside. We can ask God to help us see beyond outside things to know what people are really like.**

Which Is Which?

Peel several apples and potatoes and cut them into small, similar-looking pieces. Leave them in water so they don't turn brown. (This

70

can't be done too far in advance!) Put a plate of the apple pieces and a plate of the potato pieces on a table. Have children come up one at a time to taste one of each while holding their noses. Have them whisper to you which is the potato and which is the apple.

After everyone has tried each one, have them vote on which is the apple and which is the potato. Ask:

● **Was it hard to tell the difference? Why or why not?**

● **Is it sometimes hard to tell the difference between right and wrong? Explain.**

● **Can good and evil sometimes look the same? Explain.**

Read aloud Genesis 2:16-17 and 3:1-7. Ask:

● **Was it difficult for Adam and Eve to tell the difference between right and wrong? Why or why not?**

● **When Adam and Eve disobeyed God, did their actions help them become wise, as the serpent had promised?**

● **How can we know the difference between right and wrong?**

Say: **God's Word helps us know the difference between right and wrong. As we believe and obey God, we will be wise.**

Which Way?

Have the class work together to design an obstacle course around the room. Use chairs, tables, wastebaskets, or other objects to create at least four obstacles. After the course is set up, form pairs. Give each pair one blindfold. Explain that each pair will have one member blindfolded and will move together through the course. At each obstacle, the blindfolded partner is to decide which way the pair is to go. The seeing partner can agree, disagree, or even quietly move something so the "wrong" way becomes a better way. Have the seeing partner lead the blindfolded partner to the next obstacle and repeat the process.

As each pair goes through the course, the blindfolded partner may not necessarily know which choice to make. Continue until all the pairs have gone through the course. Afterward, ask:

● **How did you feel about the choices your partner made for you?**

● **When were the choices wise ones? When were they unwise?**

● **Do you ever feel that it's hard to see which way to go when you're trying to make a decision? Explain.**

Say: **Listen to what the Bible says about how God uses his wisdom.**
Read aloud Psalm 104:24. Ask:

● Why did God need wisdom to create everything?

● How can God's creative wisdom help you when you feel blind-folded in decision making?

Say: **When God made the earth, he made lots of decisions about colors, shapes, and more. Wisdom guided God. You can be guided by God's wisdom in all your decisions, too.**

Wise Up

Form groups of five. Give each group a rope and four blindfolds. Have four members of each group put on the blindfolds. Instruct each seeing group member to hold one end of the rope, then have the other group members grab the rope. Tell the seeing group members to lead their groups around the room for three minutes.

Say: **Listen to what the Bible says about how we can get wisdom.** Read aloud James 1:5-8. Ask:

● **What happened when everyone followed your leader? when they didn't follow?**

● **What made it easy to trust your group leader? What made it difficult?**

● **What do these verses tell us to do when we need wisdom?**

● **How can we trust God totally when we ask for wisdom?**

Say: **God wants to give us wisdom. God encourages us to ask him for wisdom. When we ask God for wisdom, God promises that he will give it to us.**

EXTRA MILE IDEA

Treasure Chest Giveaway

Photocopy and cut apart the "Precious Metals and Gems" handout (p.74) so that each child has a set of pre-cious metals and gems.

Write on separate sheets of paper five things kids might like to buy, such as a trip to Disney World, in-line skates, a new house for their parents, or season tickets to their favorite team's games. Write "wis-dom" on a sixth sheet of paper. Tape the papers to the wall.

Hold an auction and have kids bid on the items with their precious metals and gems. Save wisdom until the very end. As kids bid on wisdom, don't allow any of them to buy it. Keep saying: **No! That's not enough!**

Afterward, read aloud Job 28:12-23. Ask:

● **If we can't buy wisdom, where can we find it?**

Say: **Now that we know that wisdom can't be bought, let's look for it.**

Give kids five minutes to search the room for wisdom. Have nothing hidden but keep your Bible in plain view, possibly on your lap. After five minutes, gather the class back together. Read aloud Job 28:23. Ask:

● **If God knows how to find wisdom, how can we find out that wisdom?**

Say: **God has revealed much of his wisdom to us in the Bible. As we read God's Word, listen to the teaching of God's Word, and study God's Word, we'll discover God's wisdom for every area of our lives.**

Precious Metals and Gems

GOLD (Job 28:15)	SILVER (Job 28:15)	ONYX (Job 28:16)
SAPPHIRES (Job 28:16)	**CRYSTAL** (Job 28:17)	**CORAL** (Job 28:18)
JASPER (Job 28:18)	**PEARLS** (Job 28:18)	**TOPAZ** (Job 28:19)

Chapter Nine

Our Unchanging God

The one constant in a child's life is change. Yesterday John was my best friend, but today he hates me. Five years ago my parents promised they'd stay together forever, but now they're divorced. It's tough to figure out who to trust.

You can offer kids this encouragement: God never changes. From the beginning of time to the end of time, God will be the same. If God says he will do something, he will do it. God never lies, and he never changes. He is always the same.

Children will enjoy discovering that God is someone they can trust completely. Use this chapter to introduce them to our steadfast God.

● ● ●

Always the Same

Mark off boundaries within a large playing area. If the area is enclosed by walls, mark boundaries about three feet from the walls. Form two teams—Sharks and Tigers. Have teams stand at opposite ends of the designated area. (This game is best played outside but can be played inside as well. If played inside, have kids walk rather than run to tag a player.)

Say: **On "go," the Sharks are to tag as many Tigers as possible. Tigers who get to the opposite end without being tagged are safe. When I call out "Tigers," the game changes and Tigers are to tag Sharks. Tagged players must go to a designated corner, but they're automatically freed when the teams change roles. When I call out new ways to play the game, you must play as I say.**

Start the game. Periodically call out new ways to play such as "run (or walk) backward," "hop on one foot," or "tag with your elbow instead of your hand."

Afterward, ask:

● **What was it like to change from being a tagger to the one being tagged?**

● **This game was always changing. What things in your life keep changing at home? at school? with friends?**

Say: **Everything around us may change, but God never changes.** Read aloud Malachi 3:6. Ask:

● **How do we know that God never changes?**

● **How does it make you feel to know that God never changes?**

● **How would things be different if God changed all the time?**

● **How important is it to you that God is unchanging? Explain.**

Say: **We don't have to fear that God will change from day to day. He is always the same. The Bible teaches that God is "the same yesterday, today, and forever"** (Hebrews 13:8). **We can feel safe knowing that God will always be good, loving, and powerful.**

Bubblin' Over

Before class, make a bubble solution by adding one part mild liquid detergent to three parts water. Add one to two tablespoons corn syrup and stir gently. You'll also need a large, shallow dish and soft, pliable wire such as floral wire.

Pour the bubble solution into the large, shallow dish. Give each child a piece of pliable wire. Say: **I'm tired of round bubbles and want to see bubbles of different shapes. Twist your wire into a different shape, such as a triangle or square, then dip the wire into the bubble solution to make a new bubble. Make sure your wire shape doesn't have any rough edges.**

Have the children wave or blow through their dipped wires to try to create shapely bubbles.

After kids notice that their bubbles are always round, no matter what, say: **Sorry! You can't get creative with bubble shapes. Bubbles are always round.**

Have kids form bubbles again. This time, see who can make the biggest bubble. Kids may want to do this for a while!

After a few minutes of bubble fun, have the children sit in a circle. Say: **Just as we can't change the shape of bubbles, we can't change God.**

God has always been and always will be the same. God never changes.
Read aloud Isaiah 26:4. Ask:

- Why is it good that God is unchanging and eternal?
- What do we see in our lives that shows us that God doesn't change?
- How do people change from day to day?
- How would it affect your faith if God changed the way people change?

Give each child a small rock. As you hand a rock to each child, say: God is our rock who never changes. Have each child respond, "Praise God, who stays the same forever and ever."

Changed

Form four equal teams. Have the teams line up at one end of the room. At the other end of the room, place several articles of clothing for each team. Make sure teams have the same number of clothing pieces in their piles. On "go," have one person in each team race to the clothing pile, put on the clothing, take it off, and race back to the team. Have the next person in line repeat this process. Continue until everyone has had a turn. After the race, ask:

- How many times a week do you change clothes?
- How many times a year does God's creation change its "clothes"?

Read aloud Hebrews 1:10-12. Ask:

- What things in this world won't last forever?
- How is God different from the things he has made?

Say: God is unchanging. He is the same yesterday, today, and forever. While everything around us may change, we can be confident that our God stays the same.

Copy Me

Form two teams and have them line up. Tell the first word (see below) to the first person in each line and have them convey that word to the persons behind them by using actions only—no words. Have the second person in each line pass the word to the next person in the same way and so on. As soon as the last person in line receives the message, have him or her write the word on a chalkboard. Have the first person move to the end of the line. Repeat this process until all the words are written on the chalkboard. Then tell kids the correct words. Use the following words in this activity: hop, love, jump, dance, and sing.

Say: **Some of our words changed, but God's Word never changes.** Read aloud Isaiah 40:8. Then ask:

● **Why did the message change as it went from the first person to the last person?**

● **Can you find anything around you that never changes?**

● **How can God's Word stay the same forever?**

● **If the Bible never changes, what does that tell us about the Bible's Author?**

● **How does knowing that God and his Word will never change affect your faith in God?**

Say: **God's Word never changes because God never changes. We can trust God's Word to help us when we have problems because God stays the same and so do his guidelines for us.**

Growing Up

Form six groups. A group can be one person. Secretly assign each group one of the following roles: a baby, a toddler, an elementary school student, a teenager, an adult, and an elderly person. Tell each group to mime someone in its assigned age group eating breakfast. Give groups a few minutes to prepare, then have each group do its mime.

Say: **Based on what you've seen each group do, arrange yourselves from the youngest to the oldest.**

After kids line up, say: **People grow up. But God is different from people. Listen to what a verse in the last book of the Bible says about God.**

Read aloud Revelation 21:6. Ask:

● **Does God get old like people do?**

● **Does God change over time?**

Say: **The Bible tells us that God is the same yesterday, today, and forever. God doesn't change. God doesn't get old. God is eternal. That means that God has lived forever and will live forever. He will never get old and die. God is unchanging.**

The Old, Old Story

Have children fold a blank sheet of paper in half. On one side, have each draw a picture of something that changes. This could be related to nature, people, inventions, or anything else. Then, on the other side, have each child draw a picture of something that has never changed. Most of the students will be puzzled and unable to come up with any ideas.

Say: **The Bible tells us about someone who never changes.**

Read aloud Psalm 90:1-4. Form groups of four. Have each group draw a sequence of pictures depicting the creation of the world on a sheet of newsprint. After the pictures are finished, ask:

● **What kinds of things did God have to do when he created the world?**

● **What does God do now to take care of the world?**

● **What does God do to take care of you?**

● **What are some ways that God is working in your life right now?**

Say: **God is the same as he was when he created our world. God never changes. Let's thank God for all the wonderful things he is doing in our lives.**

Close in prayer, thanking God for the things children mentioned.

Shadow Play

Bring a bright light for casting shadows if you plan to use this activity indoors. If you go outside, pick a bright, sunny location. Have children pose to make funny shadows. They can do this one at a time or a few at a time. Finally, let the children move around as they watch their shadows constantly changing.

Say: **Shadows remind us that everything changes. Your shadow changed as you moved around. If you were outside and stood perfectly still for a long time, your shadow would still change because the position of the sun is changing, too.** Ask:

● **What things in your life are always changing?**

● **What are some things that stay the same?**

● **How has your faith in God changed this last year? How have you changed?**

● **How has God changed?**

Say: **Listen to what James 1:17 says about whether or not God changes.**

Read aloud James 1:17. Ask:

● **What does this Scripture tell us about how God has changed?**

Distribute sheets of black construction paper, scissors, and white chalk. Have each child cut out a silhouette and write on it, "God never changes." Tell children to take the silhouettes home as a reminder that God never changes.

Unmoldable

Before class, mix a batch of "goop." You will need 1 cup cornstarch with ½ cup water for each group of four. Put the mixture into pans.

Give children time to explore the goop. Have them roll it into balls then let it melt back into their hands. Also, tell children to slap the mixture. It looks as though it will splatter like a liquid, but it won't. Ask:

- What happens to the goop if you let it sit in your hand?
- What can you create out of this goop?
- How have you been able to change this goop?
- Why haven't you been able to do much to change this goop?

Say: **Even though we can mold this goop, it always goes back to its original form. It feels like we can change it into something, but we really can't. It won't allow us to change it. Listen to what the Bible says about our unchanging God.**

Read aloud Numbers 23:19. Ask:

- What does this Scripture tell us about God?
- Can anything change God? Why or why not?
- How is your goop like God? How is it unlike God?
- Why can't we change God?

Say: **We can't change God. He always stays the same. Everything around us can be molded to be different, but not God. We can trust God to be the same forever.**

What Rules?

Form two teams to play dodge ball. (With younger children, play Duck, Duck, Goose.) Before the game begins, explain that there is one new rule: When you yell "freeze," everyone must stop and listen for instructions.

After the game begins, stop the activity every so often (more and more frequently as the game progresses) by yelling "freeze," then change the rules somehow. For example, announce that instead of catching the ball to get someone out, whoever catches a ball will be out, or instead of having a base for safety, people can be hit only if they are on base.

Changing the rules will cause frustration and complaining. After the rules have changed several times, stop the game and bring kids together.

Say: **The rules of this game changed all the time, but the Bible says God's Word never changes.**

Read aloud 1 Peter 1:24-25, emphasizing verse 25. Ask:

● **What was this game like when I changed the rules?**

● **What is it like when someone promises you something and then changes his or her mind?**

● **What do you think about God's Word never changing?**

Say: **We don't have to worry about the rules or guidelines of God's Word changing constantly. God's Word always stays the same, and so does God.**

What Will Last?

Form four groups. Give each group one of the following items: a plastic bottle, a rock, a small plant, and a glass of water. Have each group determine whether or not the item it has received will change over time. Ask:

● **How might it change?**

● **Can it change by itself, or will someone or something need to change it?**

Place a 3-foot length of yarn on the floor. Point to one end and say: **This is the beginning of time.** Point to the other end and say: **This is the end of time.** Have groups each place their items on the yarn time line, indicating how long they believe their items will last.

Read aloud Psalm 90:1-6. Make the yarn time line a circle. Explain that, as with a circle, there is no beginning or end to God. Then ask:

● **How can each item on the time line change?**

● **Will we last forever in our present form?**

● **Is anything or anyone besides God unchangeable or everlasting?**

● **How does it make you feel to know that God never changes?**

Have everyone stand around the time line. Close in a prayer of praise to God because he is eternal and will never change.

Zoo Clues

Have children sit in a circle. Choose someone to be "It." Blindfold and lead It to the middle of the circle. Say: **Turn around three times and point. The person you point to has to make a sound like some animal in the zoo.**

If It can guess the name of the player making the animal sound, It and that player trade places. Otherwise, It tries again.

After several rounds, say: **The Bible tells us about someone's voice that we'll all know.**

Read aloud John 10:1-15. Ask:

- **What does it mean that Jesus is the good shepherd?**
- **Will Jesus ever try to trick us?**
- **Does Jesus want us to recognize his voice? Why?**

Say: **Jesus' voice never changes. We can always listen to Jesus and trust him because he loves us and doesn't change.**

EXTRA MILE IDEA

Past, Present, Future

Contact children before class and ask each child to bring in a baby picture and a recent school picture. Give each child three sheets of paper—one labeled "past," one "present," and one "future." You'll also need markers or crayons, glue, tape, and small stickers of Jesus. (You can purchase these at a Christian bookstore.)

Say: **On your "past" paper, glue your baby picture and draw either a picture of the house you lived in when you were a baby or something else you remember about the early years of your life.**

After children finish, say: **On your "present" paper, glue your school picture and draw pictures of your life right now. Maybe you'd like to draw your family, your house, or your school. Draw pictures of things that are part of your everyday life.**

After children finish, say: **On your "future" paper, draw pictures of what you'd like to do in the future. You might include what kind of job you hope to have or someplace you'd like to go.**

Have children tape their papers together. Then say: **Look at each part of your collage. When you were a baby, where was God in your life?** (Hand out Jesus stickers for kids to put on their first sheets.) **Now think about right now. Put another sticker on the next sheet that tells how God is in your life right now.** (Hand out Jesus stickers for them to put on their second sheets.) **How will God be in your life in the future?** (Hand out Jesus stickers for them to put on their third sheets.)

Have children find partners, explain their collages, then tape their collages to the wall.

Bring the group together and say: **God's Word says that Jesus is the same no matter how old we are.**

Read aloud Hebrews 13:8. Ask:

● **What does this mean to you when you look at your collage?**

● **What kinds of things have changed in your parents' lifetime? Did they always have a television? a microwave? a remote control?**

● **What changes have you seen in the world around you during your lifetime?**

Say: **No matter what changes around you, and no matter how much you change, Jesus will always be with you. He will always be the same, and he will never leave you.**

Chapter Ten

Our Gracious God

Grace is "God's Riches At Christ's Expense." It is unmerited favor, a wonderful gift. God pours out his grace to sinful people because he is a gracious God.

Children need to understand God's grace to know God better. Use this chapter to introduce children to their gracious God and to help them learn how to receive God's grace for their lives.

● ● ●

Examples of Grace

Have kids sit in a circle on the floor. Ask for three volunteers. Give one volunteer an apple, another a pillow, and another a glass of cold water. Ask the volunteers not to eat, drink, or pass around the items.

Say: **The Apostle Paul tells us that God gave him grace to do good things.**

Read aloud 2 Corinthians 9:8. Then say: **Because God loves us, he gives us powerful help so we can live for him. We call that help God's grace. But that help comes to us in many ways.**

Say to the volunteers: **God's grace strengthens us. Think of one way the item you're holding is like God's grace.** Ask:

● **How does that item help strengthen us?**

After the three volunteers respond, have them carefully pass the items to anyone else who wants to respond. Then collect the items and ask:

● **What other things help strengthen us?**

● **How are those things like God's grace?**

● **Why do you think God wants to help strengthen us every day?**

Give each child an apple. Say: **Let's enjoy these apples today as a way of saying thank you to God for his powerful grace in our lives.**

Gracious Beginnings

Say: **The Bible tells us about a son who returned to his father's home after being gone a long time.**

Read aloud Luke 15:11-32. Ask:

- **What did the son do with the money he got from his dad?**
- **Why do you think he decided to go back home?**
- **What did the father do when he saw his son?**
- **Do you think the son deserved what he got? Why or why not?**
- **If you were the father, how would you have treated the son?**

Then read aloud Psalm 86:15. Say: **Let's practice being kind to someone who doesn't deserve it. Giving someone a gift is a kind thing to do. Showing kindness to others is one way of being gracious. Think of someone it is hard for you to be kind to. It may be a neighbor, a friend, or someone in your family. Let's make a special gift for that person so we can show God's grace and kindness to him or her.**

Help kids make candy cars. Use a mini candy bar for the body of the car; peppermint candies for wheels; and licorice pieces, small cinnamon candies, and M&M's for decorations. Use chocolate frosting to "glue" the candy onto the car. Encourage kids to deliver their "grace cars" to the people they thought of during the upcoming week.

Limbo Dancing

You'll need a broom handle and various small prizes or candies. Choose two volunteers and have each hold one end of the broom handle. Line up all the other children in front of the handle.

Say: **We're going to play Limbo. You will get a prize each time you're able to bend over backward and walk under the stick without touching any part of it.**

Have the volunteers lower the broom handle 2 inches after each round of play. Rotate the volunteers into the game during each round.

After the game, gather children together and give each person an additional prize.

Say: **The Bible says that God gives us gifts.**

Read aloud Ephesians 2:8-9. Then ask:

- **In the game, you had to win to get the prize. Did you like that?**
- **After the game, everybody got a prize. Did you like that?**

- How was the extra prize similar to God's grace toward us?
- How have you experienced God's grace?
- How has God's grace helped you when you were in trouble?

Say: We can't win God's grace—it's a free gift. God gives his grace to every one of us because he is a gracious and loving God.

Receive It

Choose a child to come to the front of the room. Ask the child if you may give him or her a $1 bill. If the child agrees, pull the bill from your pocket and ask:

- When will this money become yours? (The money becomes the child's when the child takes it. If the child attempts to give the money back, explain that that wouldn't be a very good example of grace.)

Say: This money wasn't earned. It's a gift from me. It's a gift of grace because this child didn't do anything to deserve it.

Read aloud John 1:14, 16. Say: God's greatest gift is Jesus. Ask:

- Why do you think Jesus is God's greatest gift?
- When does God's gift of Jesus become ours?

Say: God wants to give us his gift of grace. He wants to give us life in heaven through Jesus. But we have to receive God's gift of eternal life through Jesus. If you'd like to know more about receiving God's gift of Jesus, I'd be happy to talk with you after class.

Make yourself available to talk with children after class and explain more about what it means to be a Christian.

Secret Agents

Lay a large sheet of newsprint on the floor and set out markers. Have kids gather on the floor around the newsprint.

Say: On the newsprint, draw a picture of the last time you helped someone. For example, maybe you helped your mother wash the dishes this week. It can be anything. Just find an open space on the newsprint and draw your scene.

Make sure everyone has enough room to draw and encourage children not to worry about how well they draw. When everyone is finished, have kids explain their pictures.

Then say: Congratulations on the way you help others! I'm very proud to know so many helpful people. You know, God is like that, too. When God helps us in some way, that's called grace. So when we help others, it's as though we're God's secret agents delivering his grace to people around us. Some people in a city called Corinth were also God's givers of grace.

Read aloud 2 Corinthians 9:12-15. Then have kids form pairs, hold hands, and pray together, "God, thank you for your grace. Help me to be gracious and helpful to others. In Jesus' name, amen."

Storytelling

Begin class by saying:

Listen to this made-up story. My father has been a teacher for years. Just recently, he found out that one of his students had been stealing money from his desk. Not only that, this student had also been changing his grades in the grade book. My father knew that the student's behavior was wrong. Finally, my father called this person into his office.

Before my father could say anything, the student said, "I'm so sorry. Please, I know I deserve to get punished."

What do you think my father did? He calmly said, "Yes, that is what you deserve for what you've done. Now you may go." The student couldn't believe his ears. As the student was leaving the office, my father added, "Oh, by the way, I have changed all your grades to A's, and here is $1,000. If you need more, just let me know."

The student was overwhelmed with his kindness and said, "But I deserve to be punished, not rewarded."

Read aloud Ephesians 1:7-8. Ask:

● Who in my story was most like God?

● Who was most like us?

● What is forgiveness?

● Grace is when someone gives us something we don't deserve. How did this student experience grace?

● How has God been gracious to you?

Say: There is so much more to the Christian life after forgiveness. God will help us live the way the Bible teaches us to live. We can rely on God's help and strength every day.

Surprise!

Gather kids in a circle and ask:

● Has anyone ever given you a surprise gift? What was the gift?

● Has anyone ever given you any other surprises? What were they?

Say: **God gives his children a very special gift in Jesus.**

Read aloud Romans 3:22-24 in an easy-to-understand translation. Say: **The Bible says that God gives us grace. Grace is an undeserved favor or gift—sort of like a surprise or something you weren't expecting. Turn to the person on your right and name one thing, such as life or your parents, that you think is a special gift from God.**

After kids have shared, say: **Now we're going to prepare a surprise party for the people picking you up today.**

Form groups of four. Have groups make banners to express appreciation for the people who will pick them up. Then have group members help one another wrap empty boxes with newsprint. Make sure there is a wrapped box for each child. Have each child draw a picture on each side of his or her box of one thing God gives us every day. Tell kids to take these presents home as a reminder of how gracious God is.

Once the party preparations are finished, ask:

● **How do you think the people who pick you up will feel when they see these big banners we made for them?**

● **Why do you think they'll be surprised?**

● **How is this surprise like an experience of God's grace?**

Throw the party for the people who pick up the kids.

Throne of Grace

Before class, prepare a "throne room" (it can simply be a separate corner of the room). Place a straight-back chair in the throne room and set two small boxes, one empty and one with cards in it, in front of the chair. Each card should have the words from Hebrews 4:16 written on it. You'll need enough cards for each child to have one.

Form pairs. Help children find the book of Hebrews in their Bibles. Have partners read aloud Hebrews 4:16, taking turns reading and summarizing the verse one phrase at a time. Then have each person share a need or problem while his or her partner writes it on a blank 3×5 card. (Help children who are not yet able to read and write.)

Have partners exchange the cards they wrote. Then explain that the throne room represents the way we can go to God with our needs and problems.

Have kids enter the throne room one at a time, pray about their needs or problems, tear up their cards, put them in the empty box, and each take a Scripture card from the other box. After everyone has done this, ask:

● **What's it like when people don't understand what you're going through?**

● **What's it like to know that God always understands?**

● **Where is God's throne room?**

● **Where can you go every day to enter God's throne room of prayer and receive God's help?**

Say: **God desires to talk to you all the time about any problem you have. You can pray to God anywhere, and God will listen and help you.**

Wonder Worker

Before class, prepare two Bible-story areas in your room. In one area, place several large pieces of newsprint, crayons, and string confetti that sprays from a can. (This can be found in the toy section of most discount stores.) Set dry erase markers and a large mirror or glass window in a second area. If you do not have a mirror or window available, use sidewalk chalk on a chalkboard or sidewalk.

As children arrive, gather at the first area. Tell the story of Joshua and the Israelites crossing the Jordan River (Joshua 3:14-17). As you tell the story, illustrate it on the newsprint. Use the crayons to draw simple stick figures and the string confetti to create string hair and clothes.

Move to the second area and tell the story of Joshua and the battle of Jericho (Joshua 6:1-20). Use your resources to create stick figures again.

Say: **God graciously helped Joshua, and he also helps you. Begin to think of ways that God takes care of you each day just as he cared for Joshua.**

Form two groups. Send one group to the first area, now designated "God's Grace at Home," and the other group to the second area, "God's Grace at School." Instruct groups to use the resources in their areas to draw situations of how God's grace has helped them. For example, kids in the home area might draw God helping them not be angry with family members. Afterward, have groups display and explain their creations.

Say: **God is with us each day to meet our needs. Think of a problem area that you need God's grace and help in.** (Pause.) **Silently ask God to help you with that area.**

Say: **The promise Joshua gave his people is also for you today.**

Conclude by reading aloud Joshua 3:5.

What to Do?

Before class, photocopy and cut apart the "What to Do?" handout (p. 91).

Read aloud Psalm 145:8-9. Ask:

● **What does "gracious" mean? "compassionate"?**
● **How does God treat us with kindness?**
● **How can we share God's kindness with others?**

Form groups of four and give each group one of the situations on the "What to Do?" handout. Have each group decide how to respond to its situation in a gracious way and in an unkind way. Then have each group prepare and present a role-play of each of its responses.

Help kids plan a way to show God's kindness to others. They might make a card for someone who is discouraged, plan a visit to a nursing home, or collect food that can be shared with a shelter.

What to Do?

Photocopy this handout, then cut apart the situations.

You see **someone** *pushing* another **child** **o**u**t** of a l i n e.

What Do You Do?

There **are** *only* three **s w i n g s,** but four kids want to swing.

What Do You Do?

You're **invited** to a  but your **guest** isn't.

What Do You Do?

A bully **threatens** to *beat* **u**p a s h y kid in your class.

What Do You Do?

Your F R I E N D S **make fun** of a **girl** at r e c e s s.

What Do You Do?

The same kid is **always** left **out** at *lunch time.*

What Do You Do?

Chapter Eleven

Our Forgiving God

As children of God, we rely on God to give us the grace to live the Christian life. But we often fail. We can't seem to live up to God's standards on a consistent basis. God must be angry, or so we think.

But there in the wings stands God—ready to forgive every offense. As a popular chorus says, "Who would not love [him]?" Use the activities in this chapter to help children see their loving God whose forgiveness never ends. Their desire to know God will be motivated out of love rather than fear.

● ● ●

Consequences

Distribute pencils and paper. Have each child draw or write about a time he or she did something wrong.

Then say: **The Bible tells us that Jesus paid for our sins.**

Read aloud Romans 6:23. Have children hold their papers and silently pray for forgiveness.

Say: **Crumple up your paper and rip it into pieces.** (Pause.) **Now put the pieces back together.**

Give kids transparent tape to put their pieces back together. Ask:

● **Is it easy or difficult to put the pieces back together? Explain.**

● **Why doesn't your paper look like the original after you taped it back together?**

● **What does it mean that the payment for sin is death?**

Say: **God is willing to forgive us when we sin. In fact, God sent Jesus to die for our sins so we could be forgiven. It's wonderful to be forgiven. But often, although God takes our sin away, we still**

face the consequences of the wrong things we've done. Ask:
- Could God forgive the sin of stealing?
- What would be the consequences of that sin?
- Could God forgive the sin of hatred?
- What would be the consequences of that sin?
- Could God forgive the sin of murder?
- What would be the consequences of that sin?

Say: **God is a forgiving God. But sin can still have severe consequences. If we sin, we need to remember to ask God for forgiveness immediately. Because of Jesus, God will forgive us.**

Cover Up

Have children stand shoulder to shoulder in a row. Place a coin on the floor in front of each child. Give each child at least three 3×5 cards.

Say: **Let's see who can cover his or her coin with the cards. Hold your cards at shoulder level and drop them one at a time on top of the coin on the floor.**

Give children several chances to try to cover their coins. If someone completely covers the coin, that person can step out of line and cheer on the others.

After several card-dropping attempts, play again. This time, tell children to close their eyes. Say: **Who can drop the cards and cover the coin with his or her eyes closed? No peeking!**

After several more attempts, say: **You couldn't always cover your coins, but the Bible says that God can cover your sins with forgiveness.**

Read aloud Psalm 32:1. Ask:
- **What does this Scripture say about people who are forgiven?**

Say: **Just as some of you completely covered your coins with cards, Jesus completely covers our sins. We need to accept what Jesus did for us when he died on the cross. Jesus died so our sins could be forgiven. If you'd like to talk more about how to receive God's forgiveness through Jesus, please talk to me after class.**

Drop the Ball

Form pairs. Give each pair a wadded sheet of paper. Have partners play one-handed toss, with right-handed people playing left-handed and vice versa. Afterward, ask:

- Were you ever frustrated with your partner? with yourself?
- Have you ever been hurt when a friend "dropped the ball" or failed to do his or her part?
- Have you ever had to forgive a friend for messing up?
- What happened?

Say: **Listen to what God does when we mess up and sin.**
Read aloud 1 John 1:8-9. Ask:

- What happens when you tell God that you've done something wrong?
- When you ask for forgiveness, what are some things God will decide not to forgive?
- How many times will God forgive you?
- How is God's forgiveness different from a person's forgiveness?

Say: **Let's thank God for his forgiveness.** Close in prayer.

Forgive and Forget

Give each child a piece of masking tape rolled into a circle with the adhesive side out. Have children roll the masking tape across various surfaces such as linoleum, carpet, and cloth.

Bring kids together and look at their lint collections. Ask:

- What's on your tape?
- Were you surprised to find so much dirt and stuff around here?

Say: **Sometimes we have hidden dirt in our lives, too. When we sin or do wrong things and don't ask God to forgive us, it's like we build up yucky stuff in our souls. Listen to how Jesus treated someone who had a lot of dirt.**

Read aloud Luke 7:36-48. Say: **We could substitute each of our names in verse 47: (Your name)'s sins, which are many, have been forgiven.**

Have children tear the masking tape into small pieces, roll each piece into a small wad, and pile the wads on the floor to demonstrate that "their sins are many."

Say: **Even if our sins are many, our loving God can forgive us.**

Read aloud Psalm 103:10-13. Have children take turns sweeping their tape wads into a vacuum cleaner with a hose attachment while reciting Psalm 103:12: "He has taken our sins away from us as far as the east is from the west." Make sure before class that your vacuum cleaner will actually pick up these tape wads. If it won't, substitute a broom and dustpan. Ask:

- Why is it important that we understand that we are sinners?
- What is forgiveness?
- When God forgives us, what does he do with our sins?
- How far is the east from the west?

Say: **When God forgives us, he doesn't keep a list of our sins. He forgives us and sweeps away our sin. We are totally clean before God after he has forgiven us.**

For-Giving

Before class, wrap a shoe box like a birthday gift. Wrap the lid separately so it can be removed. Cut a hole in the bottom of the box. Cut a sheet of paper the same size as the bottom of the box and place the box on top of the paper on a table.

Say: **You can see by its decoration that this is a gift. It's a special gift to each of you that only Jesus can give. This is a "for-giving" box that helps remind us that Jesus forgives all our sins and that forgiveness is a gift.** Ask:

- Can anyone tell me what forgiveness is?

Say: **The Bible says that we all need forgiveness.**

Read aloud Romans 3:23. Ask:

- What is sin?
- What happens to people who sin?
- Can you think of times in your life when you have sinned?

Say: **Maybe you've lied to your parents or a friend. Maybe you've been unkind to someone and hurt his or her feelings. Take a sheet of paper and a marker and go off by yourself. Sit for a moment and think about a time you did something that was wrong. Draw a picture or write a word about that sin, then come back and sit in a circle.**

When everyone has returned to the circle, have children crumple their "sins" and place them in the for-giving box. Put the lid on and say a prayer asking God for forgiveness.

Then read aloud 1 John 1:9. Ask:

- When we say we're sorry for something we've done and ask God to forgive us, what happens?

Carefully pick up the box and the paper underneath (to hold in the sins) and walk to the wastebasket. Hold the box above the wastebasket and remove the paper so the sins fall into the wastebasket.

Say: **When we ask, God gives us the gift of forgiveness and our** sins are all gone!

Take the top off the box to show that the sins are all gone. Sit down in the circle and ask:

● **How do you feel about God forgiving the bad things you do? your failure to do good things?**

● **When do you need forgiveness the most?**

● **When is it hard to ask for forgiveness?**

Say: **Whenever you sin, remember that God wants to forgive you. All you have to do is tell him how sorry you are for what you've done and ask God to forgive you. God is a forgiving God.**

Message Decoded

Say: **Listen to a story about two servants who forgave differently.** Read aloud Matthew 18:23-35. Afterward, ask:

● **Who are you most like in this story: the first servant? the second servant? the king? Why?**

● **When someone has behaved unfairly toward you, is it hard or easy for you to forgive that person? Explain.**

● **After hearing this story, what will you do differently the next time someone treats you unfairly?**

Say: **Let's discover a message that God has for you.**

Form pairs. Give one child in each pair a 4-inch square of red cellophane, a paper-towel tube, a rubber band, a sheet of construction paper, and stickers. Give the other partner a 3×5 card, a red crayon, and a blue crayon. Instruct the first partner to cover one end of the tube with the cellophane and secure it with the rubber band. Next, have the first partner glue a sheet of construction paper around the tube and decorate it with stickers. Meanwhile, have the other partner secretly write "Forgive others as I have forgiven you" on the 3×5 card with the blue crayon then color over the secret message with the red crayon so it's illegible. The first partner can decode the message by viewing it through the telescope.

Afterward, say: **I think you've figured it out! God is forgiving. He forgives our sins. When we learn that God is forgiving, we'll forgive others, too.**

My Father's Land

Say: **A long time ago, a king named Solomon prayed to God, asking for forgiveness for his people. Listen to his prayer.**

Read aloud 1 Kings 8:46-50. Place two blankets on the floor about five feet apart. Hang a sign saying "My Father's Land" above one blanket and a sign saying "Enemy Territory" above the second. While rereading or paraphrasing the verses, have the children act out the following:

Begin with everyone standing on the My Father's Land blanket. Choose one student to be the one who "sins against you" and lead that child onto the Enemy Territory blanket. Have that child stand facing away from My Father's Land. Next, when you say the phrase, "for there is no one who does not sin," transfer the remainder of the class to Enemy Territory and have them face away from My Father's Land. Loosely wrap a strand of yarn around the entire group several times as you explain: **If people sin all the time, they become slaves to sin.**

Continue the narrative and direct the class to turn and face My Father's Land as you read verse 48. After the children have enacted repentance by facing My Father's Land, cut the strands of yarn and explain to the children that they're free to return to My Father's Land. Have the class sit down in My Father's Land.

Say: **Each time we sin, it's as though we're taken captive into enemy territory. However, God is always waiting to forgive us if we say we've done wrong and turn back to him. God will always forgive us and bring us home, because God is forgiving.** Ask:

● **When someone is stealing money from a mom's purse, how could that child turn back to My Father's Land?**

● **When someone refuses to help people who are less fortunate, how could that child turn back to My Father's Land?**

● **Is there anything for which you need to ask God to forgive you?**

Say: **Think of that thing and how you can turn back as I close in prayer. Father, thank you for being a forgiving God. We want to tell you that we're sorry for our sins.** (Pause.) **We want to turn back to you by doing this.** (Pause.) **Please forgive us. In Jesus' name, amen.**

Rainbow Wipeout

You'll need a clear bowl half-filled with water; a spoon; several cups of liquid bleach; and red, yellow, green, and blue food coloring. Keep the bleach away from children.

Seat the children in a circle around the clear bowl of water. Say: **This bowl of water is what a person who has never done anything wrong looks like.** Ask:

- Can you think of anyone like that?

Say: **The Bible says that everyone (except Jesus) has sinned.**

Read aloud Romans 3:23. Ask:

- Who does this verse describe?
- What is sin?
- What are examples of sins that boys and girls might do?

As children name sins, have them take turns squirting drops of food coloring into the water to represent those sins.

After everyone has had a chance to color the water, stir the water with a spoon and say: **This is what our lives look like to God when they're full of sin. When our sins aren't forgiven, we can't be special friends with God.**

Read aloud 2 Corinthians 5:14. Then ask:

- Why did Jesus die on the cross?

Say: **If we believe in Jesus and accept his forgiveness, Jesus will blot out our sins and we can be clean and pure before God.**

Pour several cups of liquid bleach into water. Say: **When we ask, Jesus will add his love and forgiveness to our lives.**

Stir the water and say: **The sin is gone!** (If children point out that the water is not completely clear, talk about how the consequences of sin may remain with us even after God has forgiven us.)

Ask the children to bow their heads in prayer, then say: **Isn't it great to know that Jesus is always ready to forgive our sins? Let's thank him for forgiveness right now. Dear Jesus, thank you for forgiving us for every sin we do. Amen.**

Shoulder Push

Before class, draw three large concentric circles on the ground. If necessary, form the circles on the floor with masking tape. The smallest circle should be large enough so that all the children can stand inside it. Label the smallest circle "heaven," the middle circle "forgiving zone," and the largest circle "unforgiven zone."

Have all the children stand in the heaven circle and wrap their arms around their own midriffs. Instruct children to use their shoulders to push others out of the circle. The people who are pushed into the forgiving zone should continue pushing others to the unforgiven zone. People in the forgiving zone can try to return to the heaven circle, but children pushed into the unforgiven zone must stay there with their arms in the air. Continue the game until only two people are in the heaven circle.

Say: **Listen to what God's Word says pushes us away from him.** Read aloud Isaiah 59:1-2. Then ask:

- How can our sins separate us from God?
- How is this game different from God's forgiveness toward us?
- In real life, what can push us away from God?
- What do we need to do to get close to God again?
- How do you feel when you're forgiven by God?

Say: **Sin is ugly to God. He doesn't even want to look at it. So when we sin, we're separated from God. But our God is forgiving. As soon as we tell God that we're sorry for what we've done, God forgives us.**

Then and Now

Say: **Matthew 18:23-35 is one of Jesus' stories that's called a parable. This parable is about forgiveness.**

Read aloud Matthew 18:23-35. Then form two groups. Have one group create a skit based on this parable as though it were happening in Jesus' day. Have the other group create a skit as though it were happening today. As the groups work, answer any questions kids might have about the parable.

When groups are ready, have them present their skits. Ask:

- **The king in this story represents God. What did the king do that shows us that God forgives?**
- **The servants in the story represent us. What did the king want the first servant to do to someone who owed him money?**

Say: **Since God forgives us when we do wrong, he wants us to forgive others when they do wrong things to us.**

Have children think about someone who has hurt them in some way. Close in prayer, leading children silently to ask God to help them forgive others because he forgives us.

Undeserved

Arrange the room to play Musical Chairs. Before the game begins, tell children that there's one important rule you want them to follow: **Do not touch the chairs with your feet or hands in any way.** Tell kids that there's a prize for the winner. Then proceed to play the game normally, without mentioning the rule again. Throughout the game, keep a mental record of the person who touches the chairs the least (in all likelihood, it will be the first person out of the game).

At the end of the game, announce that the winner is not the person who stayed in the longest but the person who touched the chairs the least. Award the prize to that person and allow time for the surprise to sink in.

Bring the group together and ask:

● **How did you feel when I awarded the prize to** (name) **rather than to** (name)**?**

● **Did you think this game was fair?**

● **How do you feel when you see someone do something wrong and not get in trouble for it?**

● **How do you feel when you do something wrong and don't get in trouble for it?**

● **Is there anyone you think God shouldn't forgive?**

Say: **God's Word tell us that anyone can be forgiven.** Read aloud Psalm 130:3-4.

Say: **God forgives us even when we don't deserve it. Just as** (name) **got the prize even though he (or she) didn't stay in the longest, God forgives people even when we don't think they should be forgiven. He is full of forgiveness for us.**

EXTRA MILE IDEA

Freeze Frame Drama

Read aloud Luke 15:11-32. Help children list all the key events in order and the characters in each event. Determine what each character was doing during each event. Each event will be one freeze frame in the drama. Choose volunteers to play each character in each frame. Practice each frame in sequence, arranging characters in position. Once in position, each character is to hold that position as if frozen. Once all the frames have been determined, have kids "retell" the story by standing still in each frame for one minute. After all the frames have been presented, ask:

● **Who do you think this story is about?**

● **Which character is most like you?**

● **Why was the older son angry?**

● **If you had been him, how would you have felt?**

● **How did the father show compassion and forgiveness?**

● Do you think the younger son deserved to be treated as he was? Why or why not?

● How is the father like God?

Use your freeze frame drama as an outreach at a local park, a mall on a Sunday afternoon, or some other place, such as outside a restaurant, where a lot of people gather. Have your children set up their freeze frame drama for five-minute segments. As people ask questions, have other children explain the story and tell people that God is a loving Father who'll forgive our sins.

Chapter Twelve

Our Faithful God

When children begin to understand how wonderful it is to know God, they can be gripped by a desire to hang on tight and never let go of God. But until children realize that God is holding on even tighter, their relationship to God may be marked by insecurity: "What if I let go?" "What if I'm not a good enough Christian?" "What if I commit the unpardonable sin?"

It is incredibly freeing to discover that God is a faithful God who is committed to us for the long haul. Use this chapter to help your children understand that God is faithful. As the Scriptures teach, he will never leave or forsake us!

• • •

Back-Up

Have kids stand in a line from the shortest to the tallest. Then have kids of similar size form pairs and sit on the floor. On the count of three, have kids try to be the first in their pairs to jump up without using their hands.

Next, have pairs sit back to back with their elbows interlocked. On the count of three, have partners get up by pushing against each other.

Play again, but this time combine pairs into groups of four. Afterward, ask:

● **How difficult was it to get up by yourself? with others?**

Instruct kids to rejoin their original partners and take turns pulling each other up by the hand. Ask:

● **Was your partner more helpful this time? Why or why not?**

Say: **The Bible says that you have a special helper.**

Read aloud Isaiah 41:13. Ask:

- Which part of this activity was most like God's help: when you worked alone? when you worked back to back? when your partner gave you a hand?
- According to this Scripture, what is God doing for us?

Say: **God is faithful and will back us up in our everyday situations. When we lean into him, he leans into us. God faithfully gives us a hand and helps us when we need help.**

Choices, Choices

Put a "yes" sign on one wall and a "no" sign on the opposite wall.

Say: **I'd like you to make some choices for me today. If your answer is yes, please stand under the "yes" sign. If your answer is no, please stand under the "no" sign. Please go to either one side or the other. You must make a choice.**

Pause after each question to allow children time to move to either side of the room. Ask:

- Is red your favorite color?
- Do you play an instrument?
- Do you like school?
- Do you go to worship every week?
- Have you hurt anyone this week?
- Do you ever get angry with your parents?
- Have you ever hit someone?
- Is all your homework done?
- Have you ever been rude to your teacher?
- Do you like to read?
- Have you ever been mean to your best friend?

Have kids sit down in their last groups. Say: **In your group, talk about the choices you made and why you made them. Talk about which choices you felt good about.**

After three minutes, ask:

- Which decisions did God help you make?

After the group discussions, say: **God gives us the freedom to make choices. We can say yes or no to decisions. Sometimes we make good choices; sometimes we make poor ones. God wants us to make good decisions.**

Read aloud Jude 24-25. Ask:

- How can God keep us from stumbling or falling?
- How can you ask God to help you make good decisions?

Say: God is faithful. God will help you because he is committed to helping you do the right thing. All you have to do is ask him to help.

Follow Me

Form pairs and have partners take turns leading.

Say: Leaders can give directions for their partners to follow for two minutes. Leaders must promise to say something nice to their partners, such as "good job" or "way to go," after each completed stunt. To avoid tasks that are too hard or embarrassing, leaders must be able to perform the tasks themselves.

After two minutes, have partners switch places and play again. Then ask:

- What does it mean to be faithful to someone?
- How were the leaders faithful to the followers?
- How were the followers faithful to the leaders?
- Was it hard to be faithful and listen to your leader for two minutes? Why?
- Why is it important for leaders to be faithful?

Say: There's a man in the Bible who was asked to be faithful to his leader. No matter how crazy or hard the request, the man was to stay faithful and follow the leader's directions. In return, the leader said he would also be faithful to the man. His leader asked him to build a large ark to hold two of every kind of animal in the world. The job took him years and years to complete, but this man never lost faith in his leader. The leader also never lost faith in the man. Does anyone know who this man and his leader were?

Paraphrase the story from Genesis 6:9- 8:22. Ask:

- How did God show his faithfulness to Noah?
- Do you think God will stay faithful to you for your entire life? Why or why not?
- How can we know that God will keep all of his promises to us?

Pray: Dear God, thank you for being faithful to Noah, and thank you for being faithful to us. We'll try to be strong and faithful to you just as you are always faithful to us.

I Promise

Ask children to name some of the promises they see and hear in TV commercials. For example, a certain toothpaste company may promise whiter teeth or a shoe company may promise that wearing its tennis shoes will make people better athletes.

Show kids a container of sunscreen. Make sure the container carries a promise that the sunscreen will stay on and not wash off for some length of time. Point out the promise to kids.

Say: **You could say that this sunscreen is faithful. It keeps its promise and stays with you when you use it.**

Call for volunteers to test the product. Let several children dab sunscreen on their noses. Then give each of these children a pair of swimming goggles or sunglasses to wear. (Don't cover their noses!) Give them squirt guns and have them try to wash the sunscreen off each other's noses with the squirt guns. After the squirt guns are empty, let the observing children determine if the sunscreen was faithful to its promise. Ask:

● **How is God like the sunscreen? How is God different from the sunscreen?**

● **God is faithful. How has God shown his faithfulness to you?**

Read aloud Psalm 37:28. Then give children tiny dabs of sunscreen to rub on their noses.

Have children create a cheer to tell others about God's faithfulness. Say the cheer together and praise God by applauding his faithfulness.

Let's Make a Deal

Before class, turn three shoe boxes upside down and write on them the numerals 1, 2, and 3. Set the shoe boxes upside down on a table. Place under two of the boxes things that are better than a piece of candy, such as bigger pieces of candy or money. Place under the third box something that is worse than a piece of candy, such as a pile of rocks or an empty soft drink can.

Give each child a piece of candy. In the same manner as the host of the TV game show *Let's Make a Deal*, stand behind the table and make deals with the kids. Try to get kids to trade their candy for what's under one of the boxes. Warn them that they may get something good but they also may get something bad. It's OK if kids choose not to trade. While kids are deciding, ask: **Don't you trust me?** After everyone has had a chance

to choose one of the boxes, show them what they've traded for. Ask:
- Was it easy or difficult to make a decision? Explain.
- Was it easy or difficult to trust me? Explain.

Say: **Listen to what the Bible says about God's trustworthiness.** Read aloud Psalm 89:1-8. Ask:
- If God had been standing up here trying to get you to make a deal, would it have been easier to trust him? Why or why not?
- Would God have tricked you with a bad box? Why or why not?

Say: **When we say that God is faithful, we are also saying that God is true to who he is. The Bible says that God cannot lie. God is faithful and never changes from one moment to the next. We can trust God because he is faithful.**

No Letdown

Have kids stand in a large circle. Blow up a balloon and toss the balloon into the circle.

Say: **Don't let the balloon fall to the floor. You may only bat at the balloon with your hands. No one is allowed to catch it. As the balloon goes from person to person, count by 10s until you reach 1,000. If the balloon falls, start again and continue counting where you left off. The game ends when the group reaches 1,000.**

After the game, ask:
- How did we sometimes let the balloon down?
- How do we sometimes let other people down?
- Is it hard to keep promises that we make? Why or why not?
- Can you depend on people who don't keep promises?

Say: **The Bible says we can depend on God.** Read aloud Deuteronomy 7:9. Then ask:
- Can you depend on God? Why?
- How would you define "faithfulness"?
- How is God faithful to us?
- How long is God faithful to us?

Say: **A thousand generations is a very long time. God's faithfulness will be around even for our great-great-great-grandchildren's great-great-great-grandchildren and on and on.**

Promise Keeper

Before class, make colored salt by mixing one part dry tempera paint with two parts salt. Make red, blue, yellow, green, orange, and purple salt.

Say: **The Bible tells about a special, colorful promise God made.**

Read aloud Genesis 9:8-17. Say: **A covenant is an agreement between two or more people. These people promise not to break their agreement or promise.** Ask:

● **What was God's agreement, or covenant, with Noah?**
● **How has God kept his covenant with Noah?**

Say: **Listen to what the Bible says about God's faithfulness.**

Read aloud Psalm 119:90 and 1 Thessalonians 5:24. Ask:

● **How can you know that God is faithful?**

Help children use paper plates, liquid glue, spoons, and cotton swabs to create salt rainbows. Have each child use a cotton swab and glue to "paint" an arch onto a paper plate. Then have each use a spoon to sprinkle on one of the colors of salt. After each child shakes off any excess salt, have him or her paint another arch and sprinkle a different color of salt. Have kids continue this process until their rainbows are complete. Poke holes in the tops of the plates and add yarn hangers.

Afterward, say: **Use your rainbow as a reminder that God is faithful. When God makes a promise to us, he keeps it.**

Strong and True

Mark starting and finish lines about eight feet apart on a wall in your classroom. Provide two or three 8-inch lightweight balls. Demonstrate how to press the ball against the wall with your abdomen, then roll it along the wall without using your hands by turning from front to back. Have children take turns rolling a ball along the wall to the finish line. As soon as one child completes half the course, have another child begin.

Afterward, ask:

● **If the ball dropped, who moved: the wall or you?**
● **Could you say that the wall was faithful?**
● **What does "faithful" mean?**

Say: **To be faithful means to always be there. The Bible says that God is faithful. God is always there for us—just as the wall was always there for you. Listen to what the Bible says.**

Read aloud Matthew 28:20b. Ask:

● **If you can't see God, how do you know God will be there for you when you need him?**

● **How long does the Bible say that God will be with you?**

● **Will God be with you tomorrow? when you're a teenager? when you're old and gray?**

As each child leaves, paraphrase Matthew 28:20b using the child's name: **Remember** (child's name), **God is with you always, even to the end of the age.**

Walking on Water

Place sheets of paper on the floor about one foot apart, stretching from one side of the room to the other. Have kids stand against one wall. Ask:

● **Who can walk across the room on these sheets of paper without touching the floor?**

Let anyone who volunteers try it. Then remove every other sheet of paper. Ask again and repeat the process.

Remove every other sheet again so the distance between papers is much greater. Ask again and see who will volunteer. Let volunteers try.

Then read aloud Matthew 14:22-33. Ask:

● **How was walking on many sheets of paper like walking on solid ground?**

● **How was walking on few sheets of paper like walking on water?**

● **What did it take for you to be willing to walk on few sheets of paper?**

● **What did it take for Peter to walk on water?**

Say: **Both adventures took faith. You had to have faith in your abilities, but Peter had to have faith in Jesus Christ's faithfulness to help him. You can trust God to help you, too.**

The Rock

Do this activity in a sandbox in your churchyard or at a park. You'll need a pitcher of water.

Say: **Today we're going to do an activity to learn what being faithful means. To be faithful means to stick to something without giv-**

ing up for any reason. The Bible says being faithful is like being a rock.

Have each child find a rock and hold the rock in one hand and sand in the other hand. Read aloud Deuteronomy 32:3-4. Say: **Think about why God would compare himself to a rock.**

Walk around and pour water into children's hands. Afterward, ask:

- **Which is still completely in your hand: the rock or the sand?**
- **Which one was easier to hold on to?**
- **Which one did not change?**
- **How is God like this rock?**
- **Which one would you rather build a house on?**

Say: **The Bible tells us about two people who built houses on dif-ferent foundations.**

Read aloud Matthew 7:24-27. Lead children in singing "The Wise Man and the Foolish Man."

Say: **God is faithful. That means God is solid, firm, and unchang-ing. God is committed to being there for you whenever you need him. Nothing can make God go away.**

Scripture Index

Evaluation of *Helping Children Know God*

Please help Group Publishing, Inç., continue providing innovative and usable resources for ministry by taking a moment to fill out and send us this evaluation. Thanks!

● ● ●

1. As a whole, this book has been (circle one):

Not much help   Very helpful

1   2   3   4   5   6   7   8   9   10

2. The things I liked best about this book were:

3. This book could be improved by:

4. One thing I'll do differently because of this book is:

5. Optional Information:

Name _____

Street Address _____

City _____ State _____ Zip_____

Phone Number _____ Date_____